D0197594

Thirty-Year Plan

*Thirty Writers on What We Need
to Build a Better Future*

EDITED BY JENNIFER SAHN

ORION

Orion Readers are published by *Orion* magazine.

© 2012 The Orion Society

Orion
187 Main Street, Great Barrington, Massachusetts 01230
Telephone: 888/909-6568
Fax: 413/528-0676
www.orionmagazine.org

Design by Hans Teensma/Impress

Cover Image: "The Rare Flower," 2010
Painting by Kevin Sloan, www.kevinsloan.com

ISBN: (print): 978-1-935713-06-7

ISBN (e-book): 978-1-935713-07-4

Dedicated to M.G.H. Gilliam

CONTENTS

FOREWORD

AT THIS MOMENT IN HISTORY it is reasonably well accepted that some changes must be made to the way many of us humans inhabit the planet. Replacing fossil fuels is an oft-cited necessity, but there are other pressing needs. And when it comes to what's regarded as "pressing," we've tended to think in terms of a hundred-year horizon, or fifty at best. Yet every time a new study comes out, it seems the window closes a little bit more.

The climate models are scarier than ever. The prevalence of cancer, asthma, and other public health epidemics is unprecedented. As millions of people fight for basic human rights, multinational corporations are increasing their control over food and water supplies around the globe. Given all these facts, as well as others too numerous to list here, it seems clear that today's children will grow up in a world of diminished opportunity. But what about their children? How fast could things unravel if these many crises are left unchecked? Thirty years would be a safer bet, if we want to be handing down a planet that's still relatively intact. That's roughly one generation: between now and when today's children are having children of their own. It is not very much time.

Setting a thirty-year deadline for meaningful change has some significant implications. It means there's no more time for arguing or hoping others will figure out how to fix things.

It means today's adults can no longer foist these challenges onto future generations. It means change is no longer something that needs to happen in the abstract future. The time for change is now.

When considering the necessary shift toward a more durable future, many will assume that technology and policy instruments are the logical place to start. But one thing we may need more than anything is courage: to face the facts and do what's right. More solar panels will likely improve our prospects, but things like kindness and grace are going to be equally essential. In the long run, the world we are headed for should be simpler, more meaningful, and more rewarding than the frenzied, amped-up life we have now. But what will it take to get there?

In an effort to sketch out an agenda for the next thirty years—and on the occasion of its thirtieth anniversary—*Orion* magazine asked thirty writers and thinkers to describe one thing that humanity is increasingly going to need in order to build a better future, one with more possibilities rather than fewer, a world in which today's children's children can spend less time handwringing and more time enjoying the simple pleasures of life on a vibrant and enchanting earth. The thirty responses are collected here.

JENNIFER SAHN
Editor, *Orion*

Thirty-Year Plan

DIANE ACKERMAN

PRESENCE

IT IS WINTER in upstate New York, on a day so cold the snow squeaks loudly underfoot as the sharp-finned crystals rub together. The trees look like white-gloved hands, fingers frozen open. Something lurches from side to side up the trunk of an old sycamore—a nuthatch climbing in zigzags, on the prowl for hibernating insects. Squirrels have made zigzag forays across the snowy yard. A crow veers overhead, then lands. As snow flurries begin, it leaps into the air, wings aslant, catching flakes to drink. Or maybe just for fun, since crows can be frolicsome. Nature isn't fond of the straight and narrow, much as we may pretend to be and our fences and walkways insist.

Another life form curves into sight down the street: a human in thick blue parka and hood, laughing down at gloveless fingers, which are busily texting on some hand-held device. This sight is so common that it no longer surprises me, though strolling in a large park one day I was startled by how many people were walking without looking up, or walking in a myopic daze while talking on their "cells," as we say in shorthand, as if spoken words were paddling through the body from one saltwater lagoon to another.

As a species, we've somehow survived large and small ice ages, genetic bottlenecks, plagues, world wars, and all manner of natural disasters, but I sometimes wonder if we'll survive our own ingenuity. The farther we distance ourselves from the lively spell of the present—nature right here, right now, in all its messy, majestic, riotous detail—the harder it will be to honor and protect its precarious balance, let alone the balance of our own human nature.

But if we allow a sense of presence to steal up the bones and swirl through the rooms of a many-chambered heart, the planet becomes far too enchanting to ignore, and one finds oneself in a glade where needling worries soften, careers slow their cantering, and the imaginary line between us and the rest of nature simply dissolves. Then for whole moments one may see nothing but snow, gathering thick and wet along the limbs of an old magnolia, felting it in a white sweater of many arms. Indoors, even one's feet may smile to see a vase of six tulips, whose genes have traveled eons and silk roads, arch their spumoni-colored ruffles and nod gently as the furnace gusts. On the periodic table of the heart, somewhere between *wonderflonium* and *unattainium*, lies *presence*, which one doesn't so much take as engage in, like a romance, and without which one can live just fine, but not thrive.

Diane Ackerman is a poet, essayist, and naturalist and the author of two dozen highly acclaimed works of nonfiction and poetry. Her most recent book, One Hundred Names for Love, *was a finalist for the Pulitzer Prize in nonfiction.*

4

CRAIG CHILDS

A LARGER SENSE OF TIME

Sᴛ. Lᴀᴡʀᴇɴᴄᴇ Iꜱʟᴀɴᴅ stands alone in the Bering Sea. It is not as far south as the Aleutian Archipelago, and not as far north as the fifty-mile gap where Russia and Alaska nearly kiss. It is a ferret-shaped landmass measuring ninety miles east to west and ten to twenty miles north to south. It is what remains of the now sunken Bering Land Bridge.

From along the island's tundra capes, Siberian Yup'iks still hunt walrus and murre. They run reindeer around dormant gray volcanoes that rise up from the water. Yup'ik presence here dates back two thousand years. Modern artifact hunters dig up and sell carved bone hooks and harpoons and the occasional mask or figurine left by these ancestors. They say if you want to strike it rich, you have to dive down and dredge up old villages that are now off the coast. Beneath the waves, they uncover carvings and walrus tusks where people once lived on land. These new hunters are aware of how the noose has been closing, the island shrinking, villages swallowed one after the next by the inexorable rise of the sea.

You can hardly look into coastal waters around the world without finding reminders of this ongoing change. Bronze

Age villages are submerged all around Great Britain where a land bridge once connected it to Ireland. Near Florida, an ongoing National Science Foundation project has been mapping underwater geographies off the west coast, tracking former rivers that have been swallowed under as much as four hundred feet of water. At the confluences of these submerged rivers, researchers have discovered stone arranged into irrefutable evidence of human encampments dating back as far as ten thousand years.

Tick-tock, we've always been conscious of time. If you have stood on a beach counting waves washing up and back, you have been aware of the clock around you. But our perception of it changes. Our field of vision widens. Lifting our gaze above smaller horizons, we begin to comprehend our place in time.

Prior to the Yup'iks and their many artifacts, St. Lawrence was not an island. It was just land. It would have been a high point on the interior steppe of what is known as Beringia, a subcontinent now underwater. The view from here would not have been of dark, thrashing waves, but a seemingly infinite slope of tundra. Instead of being inhabited by sea hunters, there were Paleolithic mammoth hunters living here. On the shallow sea floor where gray whales and walrus now forage, people traveled by foot just 9,500 years ago. Sea levels were about 340 feet down at their lowest. The extra water was locked up in ice.

Fossil records of corals show repeat drownings and exposures, not just the sea-level rise now taking place. Beringia is striated with evidence of the sea repeatedly rising and falling in 100,000-year increments. This pattern follows the gradual tilt of the earth's axis, which swings out and back by one degree every 100,000 years. The subtle alteration is what drives ice ages and warmer interglacial periods like the present one, forcing long-term changes in sea levels. Some researchers believe that enough greenhouse gases have been recently introduced into the atmosphere that we are now leaving that cycle. Where a new ice age should be starting up soon, according to the earth's pacemaker, enough warmth has been accumulating that ice may not in fact return. A pattern that has been going on for at least 2.5 million years may have been broken.

Today islands in the Bering Sea are disappearing. Their permafrost hearts are melting as storm waves lash shorelines into oblivion. Pack ice has been unable to form in warmer waters, leaving islands exposed. Ancient villages are falling into the waves house by house. The world's oceans keep growing. Our warming planet hikes temperatures in the sea, causing the water itself to expand, accounting for more than half of present sea level rise. Oceans are so massive that even if global warming was stopped, it would take another thousand years for sea levels to start falling again. Seven generations seems short in this regard. At least a thousand years is now on the table. Choices made now will be broadcast thirty or more generations ahead. This is the shape of our horizon.

Craig Childs lives under a crumbling 28-million-year-old rock tower in western Colorado where he has written several books about exploring nature and time.

SIMRAN SETHI

FAITH

FOR YEARS, I implored people to swap out light bulbs and tack on weather stripping, rattling off tip after tip on inexpensive and easy ways to save the planet. For years, I demystified research and deluged people with facts, underscoring the urgency of addressing resource contamination and depletion. I highlighted bottom-line efficiencies and the coolness of green—and encouraged my colleagues and students to do the same. "Detail the cost savings, make sound scientific arguments, and embrace the trend," I'd say. "But whatever you do, please do not exhort people to act because it's the right thing to do."

That was a mistake.

Environmentalism is about more than market share and data sets; it's about our relationship with and responsibility to our world, to each other, and to what we hold sacred. Deep within, we know this is true. We experience a sense of something greater than ourselves when a sunset leaves us breathless—or a deer crosses our path. When a tree bears fruit, we are humbled, acutely aware of our place in the order of things and our reliance on the world around us.

Studies consistently indicate nearly 89 percent of Americans identify as having some connection to faith and spirituality—a number that is significantly higher than rates of participation in recycling or belief in climate change. Perhaps the most effective and enduring way to inspire people to care for our planet is not to appeal to their wallets, but to appeal to their—or, rather, to *our*—better selves.

The cultural schisms we are experiencing—across political lines, socioeconomic divides, geography, race, and gender—obscure our interdependence and points of shared connection. "Us" and "them" is a false, and often crippling, divide. Working together to ensure that our communities and ecosystems are healthy and thriving can unite us in purpose. It is not an easy task, but it's a necessary one.

The ways in which we power our lives, manage our soil and water, and feed and clothe ourselves directly impact the lives of others. Seemingly discrete personal choices are embedded in a larger context and an ever-widening concept of community. Each decision reflects a deeper responsibility—and moral obligation—to those outside of our immediate circles. The preservation, restoration, and sustenance of our planet requires the efforts of all, not some.

As we find ways to achieve our shared goals, we will come to see how our efforts are not just healing the earth, but each other. Engagement with our most deeply held values should not be seen as a response to problems. It is an opportunity ripe with hope and joy—a moment to join together to honor something bigger than who we are, to create something better than what we know, and to remember always that we are mandated by our gods, by all our higher powers, to till and keep, to serve and preserve.

Simran Sethi is a professor, journalist, and advocate dedicated to a redefinition of environmentalism that includes voices from the urban center, prairie, and global community. Her work focuses on the role of ethics and values in environmental decision-making and social change.

ANDY KROLL

A POLITICS
FOR THE PEOPLE

IT WAS AWKWARD AT FIRST, like a child's halting first steps. One sunny afternoon in August of 2011, a small band of artists and activists met beside lower Manhattan's snarling bronze bull and tried forming a general assembly. Popularized by Spain's *indignados*, the "disaffected ones," the general assembly puts raw democracy into action, a leaderless community debating issues and making decisions by true consensus. Your power is your voice. For Americans the general assembly felt strange and cumbersome, and that first day by the bull it struggled to take hold. But with time and care it grew. Then it exploded.

Soon there was the New York City General Assembly, and then Occupy Wall Street, and then Occupy all over the globe. The occupiers in Zuccotti Park governed by general assembly. Each night crowds of people packed in for a stand at the "people's mike" and a vote on the protest's future. The assembly attracted diehard occupiers and passersby alike, and for so many it fed a terrible hunger for a new kind of democracy, a process not hijacked by the "1 percent" and their agents in the halls of government. Its promise to all was: Here you stand equal among your peers. Here your voice is heard.

The nation's capital, Washington DC, is occupied—but in a much different way. Members of Congress bend to the will of the wealthy and powerful, those who plead their case with the help of lobbyists and campaign checks. This is, of course, how Washington has worked for decades, if not longer. But the five conservative justices of the Supreme Court compounded matters with their *Citizens United* decision, holding that corporations deserve the free speech rights of people and so can spend unlimited company cash on elections. Today, money doesn't just talk. Money roars.

This is not a politics for the people. A politics for the people reconnects elected officials with the citizens they govern. It eliminates the all-consuming need to woo donors, the sprint from one fundraiser to the next, and instead demands that politicians worry first and foremost about what their constituents need and believe. A politics for the people means that the voices of teachers and farmers resonate as deeply as the concerns of oil corporations or Wall Street banks. And for those who would seek change from the inside, a politics for the people demolishes the barriers to office—namely, the piles of money needed just to compete.

In a people-centered politics, lawmakers working to protect the planet, build an equitable economy, educate and feed and treat the young and the old no longer answer to donors and lobbyists. It is the public good, not private profit, that informs their decisions. Special interests no longer matter; people do. Occupy, for all its faults, offered a keyhole view of such a world. And it rang true with so many Americans. The next step is taking it beyond a shoebox-sized patch of stone and earth in lower Manhattan and into the halls of state legislatures and of Congress. What we need now are politicians who have the courage and resolve to say to people: Here you stand equal among your fellow citizens. Here your hopes, fears, and convictions matter. Here your voice is heard.

Andy Kroll writes about money and politics for Mother Jones *magazine, and is an associate editor at TomDispatch.com.*

YVON CHOUINARD

A CONSUMER REVOLUTION

WE ARE NO LONGER CALLED CITIZENS. Economists, government, and Wall Street call us consumers. The world economy revolves around our consumption. The stock market rises and dips according to our level of consumer confidence. But what does it mean to consume? One dictionary says, "to destroy or expend by use; use up." "To do away with completely," says another. A third says, "squander." That all sounds about right for how we now make our living—and how the economy works.

Yet we are still citizens with the power to create and bring down governments. Civil democracy is and has always been the strongest force in any society. As citizens, we have the power to do good; as mindless consumers, we are destroying our natural world by using up—squandering—nonrenewable resources. Americans are especially guilty because we consume 75 percent more goods than Europeans. Consumption here has become a form of entertainment, a relief from boredom that hasn't really worked for us: America ranks only eleventh or thirty-first (depending on the rating system) among the world's countries for quality of life.

I used to think that designers had the most power in a

consumer society. They decide what color clothes we wear, what cars we drive, and what our buildings look like—whether our cities look like Siena or Las Vegas. But I've come to believe that consumers are even more powerful than designers because we can choose to buy or not buy their products. The buck stops with us. We can use our power as consumers—*and* as citizens—to change society for the good instead of destroying our home planet.

To become a more responsible consumer, simply buy goods that won't go out of style, are multifunctional, durable, repairable, and recyclable. Most of all, buy less; buy what you need rather than want. The economy doesn't have to crash when we all choose to buy less, if we buy fewer but better things that are better for us. In general, goods of higher quality require more (and make more and better use of) labor. Buying higher-quality, organically grown local produce keeps your money in the community. All things being equal, buy from companies that are more socially and environmentally responsible.

But what do we really know about what goes into a pair of jeans—or what goes on inside a company? Reading a CSR (corporate responsibility report) won't tell us much. We learn how much the company gave to the local symphony, and what they've done to reduce packaging (which saves them money). But they won't tell us the bad things they're doing. The oil company won't tell us how many square miles it has destroyed in the Niger Delta, nor will the gas company disclose what toxic chemicals it uses in its fracking fluids.

Transparency is rarely something a company will offer up without being forced—or nudged. My own company, Patagonia, has its own version of a CSR report called the Footprint Chronicles, a mini-website that tracks the social and environmental footprints of many of our products. We commit to 90 percent of a product's harm at the design stage, and most of what's bad happens out-of-house—on the farms and in the mills and factories that supply us. Identifying this hidden footprint has begun to nudge us toward transparency as more questions get asked and have to be answered—and that becomes a cause for good.

Soon consumers (and investors) may have a strong new tool to help us choose what to buy or what to avoid. Over thirty-five companies in the apparel and footwear industries, representing over a third of all the clothing and shoes made worldwide, have joined forces as the Sustainable Apparel Coalition to develop a standardized tool to measure the environmental and social impact of their products across the entire life cycle. This index measures impacts from manufacturing, packaging, and shipping, as well as customer care and use, and whether the product is recycled. It allows a company to manage its entire supply chain to improve water use and quality, lower greenhouse gas emissions, and reduce toxic chemical use and waste, as well as ensure workplaces that are fair, safe, and nondiscriminatory. Eventually the index can be converted into a consumer-facing rating that will allow customers to hold a smartphone to a hangtag and compare the impact of one pair of jeans to another.

Similar efforts are underway in other industries, with over four hundred indexes being considered that will measure the impacts of everything from fish to automobiles. It's early to tell, but these indexes could create a revolution in the way we buy: they give us the information we need to be good consumers as well as good citizens—in one fell swoop of a phone.

When consumers acting as citizens choose to buy more responsibly, then corporations will have to change and governments will have to follow. That's a real consumer revolution.

Yvon Chouinard is founder of Patagonia and coauthor of The Responsible Company, *recently published by Patagonia Books.*

M. SANJAYAN

EMPATHY

I TRAVEL THE WORLD GIVING TALKS. It's part of my work, and I like surprising an audience, so my hosts usually know not to ask what I'm going to say. Often, though, they can't help offering oblique warnings about third-rail topics in their region. "Thrilled you made it," they say when I land, "can't wait to hear you tonight, but maybe you might avoid _____" and here insert "wolves" in Wyoming or "climate change" in Alabama. It's a bit of a game to me to figure out what is going to be verboten where.

When I was invited to speak at an environmental film festival in Telluride, Colorado, last year, the warning was straightforward and oddly specific. Stay clear, a local contact said, of talking about the Gunnison prairie dog, a cinnamon-coated rodent that tips the scale at just over a pound. Why she had made this admonition became clear as the airport shuttle wound east into the box canyon toward town. And it also became obvious that I wasn't going to make any friends that day.

As we drove, I mused how pretty the undeveloped valley floor appeared. The driver, who didn't look like he could afford to live in Telluride, responded animatedly. According to him, though the valley looked nice, the town had been conned into paying $50 million to save a paltry five hundred acres or so. "They got hoodwinked," he said. And now that the valley floor had been "saved," the town was squabbling about how to deal with the prairie dog that was running amok. "Look, it's all dug up," he said, pointing out his window. He was right. The meadows were sprinkled with gravel pits and mounds, with the occasional prairie dog standing sentinel. Completely protected, the critters were multiplying and eating the very expensive meadow—and to save it, he laughed, the town was now considering shooting the "rat."

The other two passengers didn't stay silent for long, and they objected. They owned second homes here, and to them, the valley floor was the soul of the community. The town had stopped development there to preserve their quality of life, they argued. Plus, the prairie dog was no ordinary rodent; it was an endangered species. And then they pulled out the heavy artillery, sprinkling their argument with words like *keystone species* and *biodiversity*. The debate swayed back and forth, two savvy environmentalists against one shuttle-bus driver, and by the time we rolled into town, our driver had tugged his baseball hat low and fallen silent. Instead of convincing him, we had simply managed to reinforce his prejudice about the privileged smugness of well-to-do environmentalists. And we, too, had failed to see anything of value in his position. Each side left hardened by the exchange.

To me this chance encounter crystallized why it's so hard to create the new environmental movement we so desperately need, one that's both inclusive and powerful. These days, the need to be right trumps our ability to listen, to really hear what someone else is saying and acknowledge it as valid. People who have never been to war talk about the war on nature. People who demonize red or blue states wonder why their ideas are being demonized. We have a suicidal streak: we caricature anyone who disagrees with us, and in the process we marginalize ourselves. Is it any wonder that "believing in" climate change has become a matter of cultural identity and not of science?

Empathy is hard. You have to be willing not only to state your beliefs, but also to hear and figure out where someone with different beliefs is coming from. We prefer the comfort of likemindedness. But you don't make friends with your friends. Instead of embracing collaboration, modern conservation has lurched between conflict and nonconfrontation. Being empathetic does not mean compromising, nor does it mean hiding your true colors. But it does mean putting yourself in another's shoes and feeling their pain, and using that as a launching point for change.

Each time I spoke in Telluride, the prairie dog would come up. My response remained the same: talk to those who disagree with you and try to understand their point of view. It's the only way to reach long-term solutions to environmental problems. After all, if this richest little town in America— where private jets are stacked at the airport like salmon waiting to run rapids—can't agree on the future of a critter that could fit in the palm of my hand, what chance do we have tackling larger issues, where the stakes are sometimes measured in human lives lost?

Without empathy, environmentalism will remain a niche interest, homogenized and utterly peripheral, and our victories will continue to be small and temporary. But if we are willing to open our hearts to the problems of others, then we just might start a real dialogue—and take the first steps toward a movement with the inclusiveness and solidarity necessary to tackle the enormous challenges we all face.

M. Sanjayan is a global environmental leader and lead scientist for The Nature Conservancy. His scientific work has been published in journals including Science, Nature, Conservation Biology, *and* Marine Policy. *He is a contributor for* CBS News.

HELENA NORBERG-HODGE

TO BRING THE ECONOMY HOME

FOR TOO LONG, people and the planet have suffered the consequences of a global economic model by which wealth is extracted for the few at the expense of the many—at the expense of even life itself. It's a model made possible by government policies that have historically favored the large over the small. Regulations, taxes, and subsidies have all been used to promote bigger businesses, more technology, more energy use, and longer transport distances.

Judged by conventional yardsticks like GDP, this global economy has been a big success; we have, it seems, been doing better and better. But look behind the graphs and pie charts, and you see a very different, and deeply disturbing, reality. Across the world, economic growth has erased diversity, degraded the environment, undermined democracy, and widened the gap between rich and poor.

We are now at a crossroads. If we want to create a liveable future, we need to rethink basic economic principles. We need to abandon the blind pursuit of so-called economic growth, which ends up benefiting only a small minority, and dedicate ourselves instead to the growth of thriving ecosystems, healthy communities, and meaningful livelihoods for all.

The essential first step in this process is to scale down and localize economic activity with the goal of meeting our needs—our basic needs, in particular—closer to home. This does not mean an end to trade—not even international trade. Insisting that everything we consume be produced within a hundred or five hundred miles is neither practicable nor desirable. But it does categorically mean an end to corporate capitalism. As it is today, giant corporations are free to roam the world in search of new markets, cheap labor, and easily accessible resources; their allegiance is not to any particular place, people, or to the natural world, but to their continuously expanding bottom line. As their wealth and power have increased, so has their ability to control the world we live in. Health care, education, the environment, the laws that govern us, even our desires and values—all are shaped by big business. In localized economies, on the other hand, businesses belong to a place and adhere to the rules of that place. In other words, society shapes business rather than the other way around.

Localization is a real solution multiplier, with immediate economic, social, and ecological benefits. Take the food and farming sectors, which we rely on in order to live. Localizing economic activity allows small, biodiverse farms to provide for local markets, which encourages farmers to increase the variety of their crops, employ more people, and use less energy and fewer resources. In fact, smaller-scale, localized production in general means less energy use and less pollution—particularly as we eliminate the redundant and wasteful shipping of identical products back and forth across the planet. What's more, reducing the scale of the economy will enable us to reduce the size of government as well—making political leaders more accountable and amplifying the voice of the ordinary citizen.

In human-scale economies, people are more connected to each other—something that, as we are increasingly realizing, is crucial to our well-being. In contrast to images of distant media stars and airbrushed fashion models that all too often promote feelings of self-hatred, anger, and resentment, role models of the future can be real flesh-and-blood people from within the community—as, of course, they have been for the vast majority of human history. And while the increasing scale of the economy systematically separates us from nature, going local will make it easier for us to experience our profound, inextricable connection to the living world around us.

Localization is already happening. Without help or approval from governments and industry, a multitude of initiatives are quietly demonstrating the potential for localized systems to provide for our needs without borrowing from future generations. So far these grassroots projects have yet to be supported by public policy, a necessary condition for a real and lasting shift toward the local. Our challenge is to replace a single, monolithic global economy with a kaleidoscope of vibrant local economies, which together reflect the extraordinary, even sacred, diversity of cultures and environments across the planet. Increasingly, this will be an economics of survival, but it's also an economics of happiness.

Helena Norberg-Hodge is the author of Ancient Futures, *producer of the film* The Economics of Happiness, *and director of the International Society for Ecology and Culture.*

SEVERINE VON TSCHARNER FLEMING

YOUNG FARMERS

AGRICULTURE LIES at the very foundation of civilization. It is a good place to start, in fundamentally shaky times, perhaps the best place to start reinventing how we do things. But who is going to do it? Agriculture may seem an unlikely career choice, an impossible dream in a nation with no frontier to create the illusion of "free land" anymore, in an economy ever less hospitable to the bootstrapping initiatives of young Americans. But in surveying the options and finding little of appeal, ever more young people are coming to see farming as both a symbolic and a concretely gratifying pursuit.

Concentration in land ownership, concentration in agribusiness, the shedding of small- and medium-sized family operations, the ghettoization of rural places and Main Street economies—these mirror the troubling trends and dysfunctional systems under critique with the Wall Street banks: the unfairness, the injustice, the impossibility of dignity in a cutthroat economy and corrupted democracy. The agricultural economy at this point is controlled by agribusiness, propped up by subsidies, oriented toward the mega, and based on cheap energy and exploitative labor practices. Like Occupy Wall Street, the young farmers movement is a cultural reaction to a capitalism problem and a systems problem.

We want to grow food. To plant trees, to hustle endless bins of produce with cold fingers. But first things first: we need land, even if it isn't virgin. The place we are talking about is America and the land that remains to be farmed is vacant lots, splintered peri-urban land, failed dairies, overgrown homesteads, abandoned land, marginal land sandwiched between areas of intense production, dry land, degraded land, and fertile but floody land. Much of America is a brownfield, contaminated by industry, industrialization, industrial agriculture, or just bad farming. But this is what we have to work with, and this is what we are working with. We don't mind concrete. We don't mind brownfields. We aren't going "back to the land" so much as we're "bringing the land back." That means cleaning up the broken glass, concrete, and crack vials on urban lots, healing the scars of erosion from tobacco farming, retrofitting manufacturing and processing facilities, protecting watersheds, planting pasture where there was corn, growing food in places thought to be vacant of the hope and the productivity we know we can instill into them.

We're willing to start out small, start out cheap, and start out only on faith. We are content to begin our training living in a tent as unpaid apprentices. To learn how to farm in a society that doesn't teach it. We are willing to start our businesses on leased land—and to work hard for equity. We know which ending we are rooting for: a stable state economy that feeds us all and that cares for our natural systems. We're interested in the process. The succession. Our practice of farming has prepared us to be patient, to wait for the opportunity and then spring into action when it appears.

But the story can't be told without a pivot point in the middle and this is the part where the power and money of the old system does not smother the power and equity of the new system. As we replace the graying generations, we cannot allow them to cash out of agriculture in a way that denies us the chance to cash in. We cannot continue allowing the whole-sale conversion of our productive land to sprawl, strip malls, mines, and export crops. At a certain point we too will need a stake in the place we are committing our lives to. We too will need to own the land, not just farm it. We can expect to repair and steward, yes, but we must also be able to expect to own the means of production.

What we have chosen to do is radical. Radical in the sense that it is hard. Radical also in the sense that it is ancient, and that its success depends on our own labor, foresight, and the wise use of our landbase. The type of farming we are commit-ted to, that sustainable kind, involves structural, biological, and cultural changes. But the way that our economy values land must also change. This project will not work if we are all tenants, working without assurance that our tenure is durable and that our commitment will be rewarded.

The choice to farm is a choice to work at the foundation of our economy and the foundation of our civilization, and from that foundation, to rebuild an economy informed by natural systems, one bounded by natural limits, that works (and feeds us) over the long haul. Don't let our rosy cheeks fool you. This is serious work, foundational work. Ancient or modern, however you see it, food feeds the cultural systems, economic systems, ecological systems that support life on this planet. Systems change; people change systems. We are the people who must change the systems. But change is not a keyboard function, you cannot cut and paste, there is no software up-date to download. It takes years to learn to farm; each lesson waits a season for another chance to come up right. The land takes time to recover from chemical abuse. One farm at a time. One town at a time. One careful pasture at a time. Fix-ing fences and barns, rebuilding mills, bakeries, cold-storage facilities, creameries, slaughterhouses, and distribution facilities. We are changing it; we are hopeful. We are changing it with our hope.

Solidarity is here, the eaters are here, the farmers are here, the generation before us is willing to train us, willing to lend us equipment, willing to share their knowledge and their marketplace. What we need now is a policy instrument that will provide a reliable avenue of access to this still majestic land. The practice of farming has already given us a taste of freedom, the capacity to make big and concrete contributions to our local place, and the courage for action. America is a land we want to commit to. We will stand our ground, once we have it. But if we don't get it, we cannot start at all.

Severine von Tscharner Fleming manages an organic farm in the Hudson Valley of New York. She is a founder of Greenhorns and the National Young Farmer Coalition, both of which represent the interests of beginning farmers.

RIANE EISLER

A CARING ECONOMY

LAST YEAR, I was invited to speak at the UN General Assembly in New York about economic development in harmony with nature. I began by saying that we can't just tack on "harmony with nature" to present economic systems, be they capitalist or socialist: what we need is a whole new way of looking at and structuring economies. That opened the way for my subject: the urgent need for a caring economy.

I realize that people do a double take just hearing *economics* and *caring* in the same sentence. But that's a terrible comment on how we've been conditioned to accept that uncaring values should drive economics. The real wealth of nations, of our world, is not financial (as we saw in the melting into thin air of all those credit swaps and derivatives); our real wealth consists of the contributions of people and of nature. Therefore we need economic systems that give visibility and real value to the most essential human work: the work of caring for people, starting in early childhood, and caring for our Mother Earth.

Yet for both Adam Smith and Karl Marx, nature was there to be exploited. For them, the life-sustaining work of households was just "reproductive work," not "productive work." This outdated approach to economics cannot help us meet the challenges we face.

There is a deep connection between the devaluation of nature's life support systems and the devaluation of the "women's work" of caring for children, for people's health, and keeping a clean and healthy home environment. The failure to value these essential activities is reflected in our flawed economic indicators. For example, Gross Domestic Product (or "GDP," always in the headlines) includes things like cigarette sales and the resulting medical bills and funeral bills—things that actually *harm* and *take* life. Oil spills are great for GDP: all the cleanup costs are added to it. Not only do these conventional measures put negatives on the plus side; they fail to include the economic value of the life-sustaining activities of the household economy, the volunteer community economy, and the natural economy.

Some people will say the value of these activities cannot be quantified. The reality is that it *is* being quantified. For instance, a 2004 study by the Swiss Federal Statistical Office showed that if the unpaid "caring" household work were included, it would comprise 40 percent of the reported Swiss GDP. Other national reports show a contribution of 30 to 60 percent. This is huge.

Yet, as documented in the 2010 study *The State of Society: Measuring Economic Success and Human Well-Being*, even most alternative measures now being developed fail to include the economic value of this essential work. This is why the Center for Partnership Studies has proposed a new set of Social Wealth indicators for inclusion in the congressionally mandated key national indicators system to be developed in the United States. These Social Wealth indicators show the enormous return on investment, not only in human and environmental terms, but in purely financial terms, of investing in caring for nature and for people starting in early childhood—in *both* the market and nonmarket economic sectors.

A major reason the economic value of these activities has

been ignored is that our culture devalues women and anything stereotypically associated with women—whether in business or social policy or in the debasement of men who embrace feminine values. This has very negative consequences for us all.

For instance, in *Women, Men, and the Global Quality of Life*, the Center for Partnership Studies compared statistical measures from eighty-nine nations on the status of women with measures of quality of life such as infant mortality, human rights ratings, and environmental ratings. The findings indicate that in significant respects the status of women can be a better predictor of quality of life than GDP. Other studies have also shown this, from the World Values Surveys to the World Economic Forum's Global Gender Gap reports.

This is not coincidental. Women are half of the population, and an underlying reason poverty has been so intractable is that women comprise the majority of the world's poor—largely because in most nations the "women's work" of caregiving is not given real value. But as the status of women rises, societies embrace more stereotypically feminine, "soft," priorities. We see this in highly successful nations such as Sweden, Finland, and Norway, where women make up 40 percent of national legislatures and both men and women back universal health care, high quality child care, paid parental leave, and other policies that give real value to caring and caregiving. Women's empowerment, worldwide, is at the heart of a caring economy. But in order to get there, we must completely reframe the conversation about economics. As Einstein said, we can't solve problems with the same thinking that created them.

Riane Eisler is the author of seven books, including The Chalice and the Blade *and* The Real Wealth of Nations. *She is president of the Center for Partnership Studies, which recently launched its Caring Economy Campaign.*

ELIZABETH KOLBERT

LUCK

SEVERAL YEARS AGO, the British magazine *New Scientist*
ran a Q & A on climate change. In keeping with the magazine's general tone, the questions were sober—for example:
"How do we know what pre-industrial greenhouse gas levels
were?"—and the answers dry and methodical: "The most in-
formative measurements have come from air bubbles trapped
in Antarctic ice." But those who read to the very end got a (not
necessarily welcome) surprise.

"So how worried should we be?" read the last question.

"How lucky do you feel?" came the response.

Luck is not a word scientists often invoke, and it's certainly
not what technologically advanced societies are supposed to rely
on. But of all the "things" that we're going to need in the coming decades, luck, I think, must rank at the very top of the list.

As the editors of *New Scientist* pointed out, one of the big
uncertainties about climate change is what's known as "climate sensitivity." Everyone agrees—and by everyone here I
mean everyone who acknowledges that the world is governed
by certain basic rules of geophysics—that adding carbon dioxide to the atmosphere will produce a planet that is, on aver-
age, warmer than it otherwise would have been. But exactly
how much warmer—how much temperatures will rise if CO_2

levels are doubled, say, or tripled—is, at this point at least, uncertain. The earth is a large and complicated place, and rising temperatures have a number of potential feedback effects. All these factors make calculating climate sensitivity difficult. This is why climate scientists construct models, and also why they always offer a range of possible futures.

If we are lucky, climate sensitivity will turn out to be on the low end. If this ends up being the case, it may be possible for societies to adjust, with only moderate amounts of pain and disruption, to the new climate we are already in the process of creating. The world will be a different place from the one we're used to, but not so different as to be unrecognizable.

But if we are unlucky, the suffering and disruption will be much greater. The world may change so radically that whole societies, not to mention whole ecosystems, will not be able to adjust. Indeed, if climate sensitivity turns out to be high, then it's quite possible we have already set in motion change on a scale that will result in social and ecological disaster.

Climate sensitivity is something we have zero control over, though it may have, in a manner of speaking, total control over us.

So, how worried should we be?

How lucky do you feel?

Elizabeth Kolbert is a staff writer for The New Yorker *and the author of* Field Notes from a Catastrophe: Man, Nature, and Climate Change. *She is a two-time National Magazine Award winner, and has received a Heinz Award and a Guggenheim Fellowship.*

NIKKI GIOVANNI

FEAR

I THINK FEAR SHOULD BE A SPICE. Something we sprinkle
on our steaks just before we put them on the grill; something
we mix in with our corn muffins and bake at 350 degrees for
twenty minutes or until golden brown. Maybe we take fear
leaves to decorate our apple pie right out of the oven . . . not
before or the leaves will burn and not look nearly so pretty.
I'm thinking if we can learn to distill fear we'll have two
wonderful preparations: perfume for smells and alcohol for
ingestion.

Perfume carries its own scent of danger and excitement,
but when we throw a little fear in there, things really heat up.
We'd have to find an exclusive outlet for it. We wouldn't want
everybody to be able to get their hands on it. I'll have to form
a committee to find that solution. Maybe the White House has
some ideas.

And if we made it drinkable we'd probably have a light
green liquid with its own two-ounce top. You can take your
fear on the rocks . . . or slip a bit of Coke in there to make it
mighty smooth. We could get the culinary channel to feature
fear at one of the drink-offs and we'd reward the best new bar-
tender with his or her very own gold bottle of fear to be used
anytime they'd like.

Maybe what will really work is we all need to have a fear tree in our backyard or a small fear plant growing on our apartment windowsill. When we are feeling uneasy we pluck a few leaves and find the right place to put them. Champagne could be the number one choice but spaghetti works too. Have a little fear once a week.

I need to explain right here, it's not fear itself that causes problems, it's when hatred is combined with it. Hatred is a bad idea. Which is why it's cheap and available anywhere you look.

Fear tells you not to lend your cousin money; don't go down that dark street, girl; take yourself home from this party now. Fear is a warning signal. Healthy. Good idea. That fish smells funny. My dog does not like this man. The planet is getting hotter. Fear is a good thing.

Nikki Giovanni is a poet, a professor at Virginia Tech, and the author of over thirty books for both adults and children. She has been awarded the Langston Hughes Medal, the Rosa L. Parks Woman of Courage Award, and the Carl Sandburg Literary Award.

ANTHONY DOERR

EMPTY POCKETS

OUR TWIN SONS are seven and lately they notice the little ®s and ™s glued onto the ends of everything. Henry squints at his cousin's t-shirt. "Life is good trademark," he reads. He looks over at me. "Life is good trademark?"

Pharmaceutical companies are running out of names for new drugs. Already pharmacists squint over linguistic minutiae: Casodex, Cerebyx, Kapidex, or Celebrex? Zovira, Zyvox, Zovirax, or Zostrix? Web companies, too, are stretching the language: Yahoo! and Google seem like reasonable names for companies when you compare them to Zazzle or Zillow or Zappos or Zumiez.

Geneticists plan to describe every gene in existence. Astronomers have already found more than seven hundred extrasolar planets. Each has been named.

Does language have an infinite capacity to describe everything describable? Probably. Does the internet? Almost certainly. But do our heads?

A medieval scribe, if he was skilled, could produce two copies of a book in a year. A bible took fifteen months to copy. A library contained three hundred manuscripts.

I have about three hundred manuscripts stacked on top of my desk right now. I have 417 on the skinny black square of glass vibrating right now in my pocket. All of Joyce and Woolf. Brad Watson's *Aliens in the Prime of Their Lives*. Conrad's novels. Twain, Nabokov. The complete works of Shakespeare.

Some hours it feels like a miracle. Other hours it feels like a cinderblock.

Believe it or not, every bit of data we create corresponds to a bit of mass. Fill your camera with vacation photos and your memory card has become infinitesimally heavier. Download a book onto an e-reader and the e-reader has gained weight: about 10^{-18} grams.

Not much, of course. The whole internet, a physicist named Russell Seitz calculated, weighs about as much as a strawberry. Still: a movie on your laptop, a song on your phone, a video on your camera, sixty-six new e-mails on your BlackBerry—can't you feel the tide of all that data climbing past your waist, rising toward your throat?

Don't fall in. The strawberry could pull you under.

Manufacturers of consumer electronics are preparing to put chips in tables and fish tanks and contact lenses. "Ubiquitous computing" is the goal: wallscreens so thin and inexpensive we can paste them up like wallpaper; laptops so flexible we can wad them up and stuff them in our pockets like tissues. Thirty years from now our kids will tap the kitchen window and watch a weather forecast superimpose itself across the backyard.

Computers in the walls, in airplane seats, in roads, in thin air.

Want to check in at work? Want to know the score? Want to watch a praying mantis eat a mouse? Simply blink your eyes.

Do we want this future for our children?

If it means they can ride in driverless, crash-impervious cars to a clinic where a doctor can scan their genomes with her telephone, predict their proclivities for diseases, and inject cancer-fighting nanobots into their bloodstreams, probably yes. Hell yes.

If it means they're going to feel like I feel after I've taken a break at work and wandered onto Facebook, where suddenly I've plunged into fractal-like, despair-inducing, oversatiating spirals of curiosities—ninety-year-olds running marathons, shocking carbon emissions data, an interview with Haroula Rose—then maybe not.

Probably not. Hell no.

What we'll need in the decades to come is clear-headedness. The strength to turn off the radio, the iPad, the wallscreen, the semitransparent microlaser-powered reality-augmenters glued to our eyeballs. We'll need to remember that sometimes the most important thing we can do is forget.

We wake up in a house on the Oregon coast. It's dawn and the sky is filmy with pale fog and the wind is low, and we decide to walk down the beach to the doughnut shop.

The dog and I leave first. Out on the huge, empty plain of low tide, everything is driftwood and sand and the jet-engine roar of the sea. The sun burns 93 million miles behind the fog, the dog charges toward the wavebreak, then stops and sniffs at a huge hank of stranded kelp, and I think of the sheaves of mussels stuck on the tidal rocks ahead of us—how when you put you ear toward them, you can hear them suck and click and whisper. The huge purple starfish with their mad clinging. The trundling hermit crabs, the galaxies of snails. The gulls drowsing on the flats. The sand shrimp in their wet burrows.

Yesterday, at the tidepools, literally quaking with excitement, my son Owen looked up at his mother and said, "Please don't let me be dreaming, Mom."

For another minute the dog and I remain alone. I stop. I pat my pockets. I realize that I forgot my phone.

A weekday and my phone is not in my pocket. What if I get a call, a text, an e-mail? What if we get lost? What if I get stuck somewhere with no Mark Twain to read?

I almost panic.

Then, suddenly, I don't.

It's coming. Soon we won't be able to leave our computers behind. Whatever information we think we need, it won't wait.

But here—right in front of you—is the sweet gift of life, to have the dark flesh of your heart deliver you two miles down a beach to a doughnut shop.

The dog comes sprinting over the dunes. Then my sons in their raincoats. Then my wife.

We carry nothing.

Anthony Doerr is the author of four books, The Shell Collector, About Grace, Four Seasons in Rome, *and, most recently,* Memory Wall.

RICHARD LOUV

A NEW NATURE
MOVEMENT

FOR MANY PEOPLE, thinking about the future conjures up images of *Blade Runner, Mad Max, The Road*: a post-apocalyptic
dystopia stripped of nature and human kindness. We seem
drawn to that flame, but it's a dangerous fixation. There are
many reasons for the attraction—global threats to the environment, economic hard times, decades of disconnection
between children and nature—but there's a fundamental
problem with it too. Martin Luther King Jr. taught us that any
movement—any culture—will fail if it cannot paint a picture
of a world that people will want to go to.

Despite its undeniable successes, environmentalism is in
trouble: polls describe a public with diminishing regard for
environmental concerns. What we need is a new nature movement, one that includes but goes beyond traditional environmentalism and sustainability, one that paints a portrait of a
compelling, inspiring society that is *better* than the one we pres-
ently live in. Not just a survivable world, but a nature-rich world
in which our children and grandchildren thrive.

Inchoate, self-organizing, this new nature movement
is already beginning to emerge. It revives old concepts in

health and urban planning (Frederick Law Olmstead, Teddy Roosevelt, and John Muir come to mind) and adds new ones, based on recent research that shows the power of nearby nature and wilderness to improve our psychological and physical health, our cognitive functioning—and our economic and social well-being. Colorado University professor Louise Chawla describes the basis of the movement as "the idea that as humans we can not only make our ecological footprints as light as possible, but we can actually leave places better than when we came to them, making them places of delight."

Among its tenets: The more high-tech our lives become, the more nature we need. Cities must become engines of biodiversity. Natural history is as important as human history to our regional and personal identities. Conservation is no longer enough; now we must "create" nature where we live, work, learn, and play. Likewise, energy efficiency isn't enough; now we must create human energy—in the form of better physical and psychological health, higher mental acuity and creativity, and by truly greening our cities.

This movement isn't about going back to nature, but forward to nature.

Who are some of the players? Traditional conservationists and producers of alternative energy, of course, but also public-health professionals and physicians who have begun to write "park prescriptions"—and ecopsychologists, wilderness therapy professionals, and other nature therapists. Add in citizen naturalists who are salvaging threatened natural habitats and planting new ones. The new agrarians: community gardeners and urban farmers (including immigrants practicing what has been called "refugee agriculture"); organic farmers and "vanguard ranchers" who restore as they harvest. Also, urban wildscapers and people who are replacing their suburban yards with native species, suggesting the potential for what botanist

Douglas Tallamy calls "a homegrown national park."

Include, too, champions of walkable cities and active living. And design professionals: pioneering biophilic architects, developers, urban planners, and therapeutic landscapers who take green architecture and planning to the next level, transforming our homes, workplaces, suburbs, and inner-city neighborhoods—potentially whole cities and their transportation systems—into restorative regions that reconnect us to nature.

The largely grassroots No Child Left Inside movement—both a subset of and a model for the larger movement—has made inroads in policy and, more importantly, has planted the seeds for self-replicating social change, including regional and state campaigns that have brought together businesspeople, conservationists, healthcare providers, and others—including thousands of parents who have banded together with other parents to create family nature clubs, which offer them a sense of safety and community as they strengthen family bonds. Add "natural teachers" who insist on taking their students outside, or creating open, nature-based schools. Law-enforcement officials who view natural urban places as a key to safer communities. Librarians who transform their libraries into "naturebraries" that serve as hubs of bioregional knowledge. And artists and musicians who lend their talents to such efforts. Stir these groups together with the outdoor recreation industry and new businesses that could make connecting people to nature a growth industry. Plus anglers, hunters, and vegetarians—those who not only consume but restore nature.

The new nature movement must be more diverse than traditional environmentalism. So, include both liberals and conservatives—from the slow food, slow family, and simplicity movements to the religious Creation Care movement. And recent immigrants, and inner-city youth, who can become the most convincing advocates for nearby nature and outdoor experience—once they get a chance to have such experiences.

Some, but not all, of these individuals and groups already identify themselves as environmentalists. They do not necessarily see themselves as part of one movement—yet. Like Occupy Wall Street at its outset, this parallel movement is short on organization, messaging, and public relations. That must change. Consider the collective power if, despite despair and the odds against the human race, these forces came together to craft a positive vision of the future, a newer world based on a transformed human relationship with nature. We don't have to agree on everything to get there. But we do need to set some compass points, quicken our pace, and begin to create the future we want.

Richard Louv is the author of The Nature Principle: Reconnecting with Life in a Virtual Age *and* Last Child in the Woods: Saving Our Children from Nature-Deficit Disorder. *He is founding chairman of the Children and Nature Network.*

JANE HIRSHFIELD

OPTIMISM

WE ARE GOING TO DIE, and everyone we love and care about will die too. Whatever we have, we'll lose, to time, to Heraclitean fire and flux. A few planetary breaths ago, much of a then-thriving biosphere vanished, by asteroid strike or some other climactic catastrophe. Some billion or so years from now, the sun will begin to change into a red giant, first heating, then consuming the inner planets, including Earth. Meanwhile, scientists now believe, an ever-expanding universe stretches toward a diaphanous thinness equally unfriendly to what's sometimes called "life as we know it."

From the point of view of that "we," it's quite certain: all will come to a bad end—creeks and cloudberry bushes, planktonic diatoms and blue whales, six-toed sloths, giant squids, bowerbirds, physicists, soldiers, pacifists, sweatshop workers, shamans, dragnet fishermen, CEOs. Even that sturdiest of higher life forms, the 100-million-year-old cockroach—gone, by fire or ice, whatever we do or don't do, however it goes in the meantime.

But, ah, that meantime. Which exists now, which will have existed even after it's vanished. In whose fragrance and flowering we live. Meantime whose end we humans seem unfathomably hellbent to hasten, in ways by now quite familiar.

There's a Japanese saying: "Even the reverse has a reverse." Might our human rush toward disaster have one, too? Mind says, "Not likely"; heart answers, "Perhaps." The fulfillment of that "perhaps" depends, in part, on some ground-note of optimism in us. As a poet, I have always turned in difficult times to an impractical curative: To the hope that some image, some word might know more than I do. To poetry's own resourcefulness, when no other rope seems near. To seek beauty amid calamitous circumstance feels in itself an act of resilience and liberation. This buoying sense that change is possible, that the world is malleable, is the beginning of art. It is also despair's reversal. Without a grain or two of optimism's antiparalytic, however irrational, who wouldn't give up, facing the next hundred years?

In darkest prospects, optimism wicks enough light to see by, enough hope to move by. As we contemplate diminishing diversity, wildlands, and freshwater, as we face climate instability, population growth, toxic soils, it's clear that human ego and will alone cannot undo what they themselves have caused. In an age of hubris, then, a realistically chastened sense of human limitation is simple, springboard sanity; a sane optimism cannot be arrogant or certain of its own outcome. We do need a tectonic change within our own psyches. We do need a renewed communal compact, at the level of species, at the level of planet. But we need also—as the mythical Psyche needed the help of ants to accomplish her own impossible task—the trees' and mollusks' resourcefulness, the scouring assistance of evolution.

To retain some trust in the earth's own reservoir of resilience, along with awareness of its frailty, is an essentially spiritual sustenance and inner enzyme. Yet all life, it seems to me, is somehow hopeful. A seed sends out its first root in vegetal hope of water, nutrients, light. A newborn's lungs open in animal trust of breathable air.

Though I use the words *optimism* and *hope* almost interchangeably here, they're not the same. A friend once defined the difference: "I find optimism a state of mind, hope a state in time." Hope is event specific, and sometimes appropriate, sometimes not. T. S. Eliot wrote in his wartime "Four Quartets," "I said to my soul, be still, and wait without hope, for hope would be hope of the wrong thing." "Hope," Emily Dickinson wrote, "is the thing with feathers." Both are right. Hope unnuanced, oversimplified, invites wrong action or inaction, yet life without hope's feathered heart-lift would be unbearable.

Unforeseeable good as well as unforeseeable harm is part of the palette of the real. If the Gulf of Mexico appears to have healed in some ways unexpectedly quickly after an event as brutal as the 2010 Deepwater Horizon oil spill, it is because unknowable actions by creatures beyond our power to harness did their own digestive, transformative work, all around and under our polyester booms and questionable dispersants. Blind optimism would mean depending only on that unforeseeable assistance, or, as unrealistic, believing in human ingenuity as inevitable savior. Pessimism untempered would mean giving up, letting the inertia of powerlessness run its toxic course. A sane optimism, though, may be part of the psyche's own life stock of unaccountable bacteria and plankton, transmuting petroleum darkness back into the carbon-based life that was its source.

The capacity for optimism allows for effort in any circumstance, even the worst. It also allows a resilient joy, past logic, past reason, to come forward and graze the heart's pastures, when logic and reason would lead only to grief. Above the oil-slicked Gulf was the glimmer of stars each night, the gold skim of light each morning. A heart still able to take joy in these, to believe that children and cormorants may be here to take joy in them a century, five centuries, from now, gives reason a reason to want to go on.

Jane Hirshfield's recent books of poetry include Come, Thief *and* After.

CHARLES BOWDEN

TO REMEMBER
HOW TO DREAM

Juárez could no longer wait for us, and so, sad-eyed, the city crossed the threshold and began carving out a future while we pretended it did not exist. It became a city of assembly plants, then murder, and, finally, a city where crime is the economy.

We have always believed we owned the future. Juárez spits in the eye of our arrogance.

Juárez today is full of poor people. Its location was determined by geography—348 years ago it was the choice crossing of the Rio Grande and linked central Mexico to its imperial outpost in Santa Fe. But the border city we see and its scale only exist because of an international boundary created when the U.S. stole half of Mexico during the Mexican War. Juárez has limited agriculture along the river because the U.S. has almost all the water rights.

This city lives the future. Juárez has no justice system— 3 percent of all murders result in the authorities thinking they know who might have done the crime. It also features a growing type of economic activity—gangster capitalism. This fusion of criminal organizations, the state, and corporations is a global phenomenon, and its striking characteristic is that it produces an even worse distribution of income than pure capitalism or state corporatism.

Here is the city: 27 percent of the houses have been abandoned, 40 percent of the retail businesses have closed, 100,000 factory jobs have been lost, 30,000 to 60,000 of the rich have fled to El Paso, 100,000 to 300,000 of the poor have fled to the interior of Mexico. The city has produced at least 10,000 new orphans and 100,000 abandoned dogs. In one month in 2010, 359 people were killed, in a year that devoured more than 3,200 souls.

In the U.S., the current moment of economic panic, rising resource prices, and global warming is used by corporations to float schemes to maintain the status quo: solar farms, orgies of windmills on the hillsides, genetically altered crops, the rebirth of nuclear power wearing a nice green glow, electric cars, everything but conservation of resources and redesigning our energy infrastructure so that it becomes small and local. Centralized power is like centralized government, a threat to human rights and the human spirit.

And we need a redistribution of work. High unemployment has become structural in the U.S. as the infrastructure of the country falls apart and as the systems for producing food, fiber, and material goods remain tied to declining fossil fuel stocks. I'll make it simple: we have people standing around idle as we face more work than we can ever possibly do. Plus, we will never have social peace until people have work. Everything in an ecosystem works, even the lion king. People don't just need work for money, they need real work to feed their souls.

The industrial nations see themselves as the sole proprietors of the future. I do not believe this. The developed nations are too hidebound to downsize or think creatively. We have become the Grand Inquisitor in Dostoyevsky's great telling: the culture that kills the Christ but does not give birth to the Christ.

The busted regions of the world are closer to the future than the industrial states because, for better or worse, they will have to improvise simple solutions or they will perish. In the city without real infrastructure, water will become cistern culture. In the city without real electricity delivery to many of its citizens, power will be solar on the roof. In a city of absolute corruption, security and politics become very local and will exist block by block, or no one will make it out alive.

I doubt the future will be an easy ride for any of us. We have almost 7 billion fellow humans on this ball of dirt, and according to the late Nobel Laureate Norman Borlaug, the architect of the green revolution in agriculture that averted vast famines in the '70s and '80s, the solar-driven production of the planet will feed about 4 billion people. He once asked, who is going to tell the other 3 billion?

Basically, the brightest minds seem to be focusing on how to satisfy aggregate demand, keep all those SUVs and McMansions humming. I don't think there is a fish in the sea, a tree in the forest, a bird in the sky, or a beast on the land that shares this goal. We can't accomplish much except death by maintaining current levels of consumption, and we can't accomplish anything at all by focusing on a single species. I realize that when anyone raises such points they are called elitists and told to think of the global poor. To hell with this cant from people who have not demonstrated much interest in the global poor until their own gluttony is attacked.

Lifeboat ethics won't work in a world of rising seas. We either fix the places like Juárez or we fix nothing. The Great American Wall going up on the U.S. border is useless in stopping global warming, much less the flight of billions of human beings. The time for gated nations has passed, if it ever existed. The king in the castle with his moat is doomed unless he reaches out to the people who will soon gather at the gate with pikes. The nuclear shield is useless against changing skies, and none of the border patrols will prove sufficient when the tsunami of starving humanity arrives at the boundaries invented by nations.

And by God, we've forgotten how to dream. We cannot imagine a solution without increased consumption by people. We cannot imagine happiness without more property. Actually, we cannot imagine happiness, so we seek out chemicals either on the street or from the doctor. We live in fear, and that single fact can kill us all. Dream, I say. Dream other ways of living, dream new joys, dream a world where you have less but live more.

The future is likely to be rough, but there will be pleasure, there will be song, and there will be love. During the siege of Leningrad, after a winter of starvation and cannibalism, survivors staggered down to the auditorium to hear an abbreviated concert by the remnants of the orchestra, because it is about saying yes, and life is about joy.

Charles Bowden's recent books include Murder City: Ciudad Juárez and the Global Economy's New Killing Fields *and* Some of the Dead Are Still Breathing, *winner of the 2010 Orion Book Award.*

JAMES HOWARD KUNSTLER

A PLAN

Bob Dylan got it right forty years ago when he sang: "Something is happening but you don't know what it is, do you, Mr. Jones?" Future shock was disorienting enough during a more optimistic era, when so many things were changing in the direction of what we call "progress." The situation today is even more unsettling, but for a different set of reasons. The first tremors of the peak oil predicament are thundering through the global economy, and we have no idea how we are going to respond. Progress itself is in jeopardy, and the anxiety is palpable.

Unfortunately, too many thinking people assume that a succession of energy resources is an entitlement of history. The popular narrative goes like this: when we used up too much wood, we switched to coal, then we discovered oil, then natural gas, then uranium. It's been such an orderly succession that there's surely another new resource waiting in line. This is more wishful thinking than sound theory. While there are many types of so-called alternative energy systems, virtually all of them depend on the existing fossil fuel economy to create, run, and maintain them. Too many people still believe that we will somehow run Walmart, Disney World, the U.S. military, suburbia, airlines, and the highway system on wind, solar, algae oil, and other wondrous "innovations." They're going to be very disappointed when that doesn't happen.

The dynamic of what we are facing is one of permanent and comprehensive contraction. Reality is telling us that we have to reduce the scale of everything we do, including our notion of how many people the biosphere can support, as well as the main activities associated with human life: food production, trade, transportation, etc. This "re-set" of civilized life (if we're lucky enough to remain civilized) will happen whether we are prepared for it or not—and we're doing a poor job of preparing.

We've constructed a massive, complex infrastructure to deliver the comforts and conveniences for daily living—the matrix of skyscraper cities, vast suburbs, commercial supply chains, hierarchical roadway networks, energy delivery systems, military protection services, and capital funding operations that have worked elegantly together to form an advanced economy. We can't imagine letting it go, and this failure of imagination accounts for our lack of preparation.

It exists alongside a comprehensive failure of leadership spanning politics, business, academia, the media, and the clergy. Surely the president of the United States is conversant with the peak oil situation and its implications, yet he has not addressed these matters at any public forum. When giving a major energy policy speech in early 2011, Obama presented several outright falsehoods as fact, including the idea that the nation could become "energy independent" while still running all the highways, suburbs, Walmarts, and other stuff. The president's political opponents have shown equal, if not greater, foolishness in their *drill, drill, drill!* invocation of limitless resources, coupled with strenuous climate change denial.

Top-down political leadership has clearly failed us. I draw a couple of conclusions from this: 1) There is no guarantee that this nation will remain intact as a unified political entity; and 2) Changes in economy and governance will be attended by a period of disorder. Apparently the official plan for a reality-based future is to improvise as things happen. We Americans have always prided ourselves on being nimble, re-silient, and brave in the face of adversity, but to have no coher-ent consensus about what we face, and no agreement about what to do about it, may strain our capacity for impromptu heroics.

It's time to recognize that, as individuals, we're pretty much on our own with this set of problems, so we should start creating our own personal plans. A top priority for yours should be the choosing of a sturdy community in a region of the country that has reasonable prospects for producing food, and that has access to water, including water for transporta-tion. North America has a fabulous inland waterway network, as it happens. Look there. Cultivate a social network of skilled people. Imagine ways that you can be useful and helpful to others and be kind to them. Remember that there are always opportunities beyond your own field of vision.

There. That's more than the U.S. government has told you.

James Howard Kunstler is the author of The Long Emergency, The Geography of Nowhere, *and other books of fiction and nonfiction.*

DEBORAH CADBURY

A MORE BENEVOLENT FORM OF CAPITALISM

As CRISES IN BANKING and the Euro spread panic to financial markets and protestors in major world cities campaign for
changes to our modern form of global shareholder capitalism,
it is worth reflecting on a lost heritage of benevolent capitalism that could inform today's debate. The scale of debt, not
just for banks, but entire countries, the recklessness of top
business leaders, and the endemic culture of self-interest: all
this forms a stark contrast to the values of Quaker entrepreneurs who created many famous businesses in the nineteenth
century.

One such entrepreneur was a distant forebear of mine,
John Cadbury, for whom Quaker idealism lay at the heart of
his fledgling chocolate business in the 1820s. He aimed to
create a nourishing new cocoa drink as an alternative to alcohol, which was the ruin of many poor families in the industrial slums of England. He was guided by a set of principles
that had been developed by Quakers since the 1700s, and that
effectively formed the first code of business ethics.

For a Quaker businessman, wealth creation for personal gain only was seen as shameful. It was believed that a business should benefit all its key stakeholders, and the love of money was dismissed as a "snare." Reckless borrowing was also condemned by Quaker elders. "Extravagant debt" was seen as a form of "thievery" that could lead—in words that seem prescient to this day—to "the wronging of others and their families." Even advertising was deemed unnecessary; if a product was honest it would sell itself. This "Quaker capitalism" might seem a heavy burden to any budding entrepreneur today, but it proved to be astonishingly successful. When John Cadbury started his cocoa shop there were seventy-five Quaker banks in Britain, one in every major city, and more than two hundred Quaker companies. Many of these became household names such as Barclays, Lloyds, Gurneys, and Pease in banking, and Clarks, Rowntree, Fry, and Cadbury in business.

John Cadbury's sons, George and Richard, were among the first to recognize the potential for the mass production of food to supply the growing industrial cities. The nourishing cocoa soups enriched with barley or lentils and the handmade chocolates of the 1830s became the world's first mass-produced chocolate bars and pure cocoa drinks a generation later. As the Cadbury business expanded, the family embarked on a long-held dream of creating a model village for their workforce, in contrast to a growing number of industrial slums. Their "factory in the garden" at Bournville, outside Birmingham, with workers' cottages nestled around a village green and cricket pitch, rapidly grew into a utopian community with schools, staff grounds, hospitals, churches, and colleges. George and Richard pioneered sickness benefits, paid holidays, and a pension scheme for staff, as well as a free doctor and dentist. It may seem paternalistic today, but workers in the nineteenth century were very eager to be a part of this aspirational community, with a real chance to improve their family's lot in life. For the entrepreneurs themselves, care for others was built into the business model.

What happened to the Quaker capitalism of the nineteenth century as global competition intensified? In 2009, America's largest food giant, Kraft, began a hostile bid for Cadbury. In the multibillion-dollar showdown that followed, independence and Quaker tradition were pitted against the cutthroat tactics of a global corporate leviathan. At the start of the takeover, hedge funds owned 5 percent of Cadbury, but as the deadline for Kraft's bid approached, this figure rose to over 30 percent. Hedge funds told the Cadbury management that they would be prepared to sell for a mere twenty-pence-per-share profit. Thus the fate of an iconic 186-year-old business and its thousands of employees was determined by people who hadn't owned the company for more than a few weeks, and who had no intention of owning it a few weeks later.

The takeover process highlights how the notion of ownership itself has changed. Today's businesses and their investors are global, and the old loyalties have broken down. There is a serious misalignment between the perceived need for international shareholders looking for fast profits, and the needs of companies to build long-term growth. All this is having a significant effect on communities. Poignant images from Cadbury's Bournville archives convey a strong sense of belonging that sprung from employment at the chocolate factory. Sports days on the Bournville cricket pitch, gardening with the Bournville landscaping department, Cadbury cocoa caravans bringing comfort to bombed-out streets—such images highlight the role of the factory in families' lives across generations.

But today, the sheer scale of global business has fragmented such communities. In the chocolate industry, the British firms of Rowntree and Mackintosh's have been swallowed by Nestlé, the world's largest food company, while Cadbury, Terry, and Fry are now part of the world's second largest food company, Kraft. Major business decisions that affect entire communities are typically made by a handful of managers working off balance sheets, often on a different continent from their workers.

This raises questions about the spirit of business. The Quaker pioneers believed your "soul lived or perished according to its use of the gift of life," and this belief informed their decisions. While few would mourn the separation of religion from business, many of us do mourn the extent to which morality is missing from today's boardrooms. Promoting community, the purposeful sharing of prosperity, the betterment of our fellow man—these may sound like quaint novelties in today's world of global finance, but as the legacy of Quaker capitalism shows, not only are such goals admirable and attainable, they're simply good business.

Deborah Cadbury is the author of Chocolate Wars.

MARC BEKOFF

COMPASSION

WHILE WATCHING ELEPHANTS in the Samburu National
Reserve in Northern Kenya, I saw a teenaged female, Babyl,
who walked very slowly as if each step was difficult to make.
I learned she'd been crippled for years and other members
of her herd never left her behind. They'd walk a while, stop,
and look to see where she was. If Babyl lagged behind, some
would wait. Had she been left alone, she undoubtedly would
have fallen prey to a lion or other predator. Sometimes the
matriarch would feed Babyl.

Babyl's friends had nothing to gain by helping her. None-
theless, out of friendship and compassion they changed their
behavior to allow her to remain with the group. Friends don't
leave friends behind.

We can learn a lot from other animals. "More science
and more technology are not going to get us out of the
present ecological crisis until we find a new religion, or rethink our old one." So wrote historian Lynn White in 1967 in
his now classic essay "The Historical Roots of Our Ecological
Crisis." Forty-five years later, White is still right. We don't
need more science to know we need more compassion.

Compassion, suffering with others based on empathy
and sympathy, will help us cross the boundaries we have

created between cultures and species, human and nonhuman. Compassion will help us overcome our alienation from nature. Compassion will be the central part of a new mindset and social movement for the future—one where we'll stop trying to outsmart nature by competing with it in desperate, senseless, lose-lose interactions.

Humans have a global tendency to redecorate nature, to move into the living rooms of other animals with little or no regard for what we're doing to them, their friends, and their families. We unrelentingly intrude because there are too many of us, because we dispassionately overconsume, increasing our "ecological footprint" when instead we must begin thinking about our "compassion footprint." We need to calibrate our sense of success in terms of the kindness and respect we add to the world through protecting animals and ecosystems rather than harming them. We're an integral part of the awe-inspiring webs of nature, and all beings suffer when these complex interrelationships are compromised.

A lack of compassion has gotten us to where we are. But if we act as a committed and concerned human community, the work of compassion will pull us together and propel us forward. It may be difficult to be optimistic, given the challenges with which we're faced. However, we need not fear running out of compassion, for compassion begets compassion. As we heal animals and ecosystems, we will increasingly find that we are also healing ourselves.

Marc Bekoff is the author of numerous books, including The Animal Manifesto: Six Reasons for Expanding Our Compassion Footprint. *He taught for many years at the University of Colorado.*

TAMAR ADLER

TO EAT
WITH GRACE

It will answer many hungers, and its design will be savored slowly.
—M.F.K. Fisher
Introduction to *Japanese Cooking: A Simple Art*

ON THE MENU that sustains us in 2040, the practical, pleasurable, and ethical will be melded. Those three qualities, which now bang and clash against each other—our squeezing food preparation tightly between other activities, a curiosity in the pleasures of the table, awareness of where our food habits and food system are fragile and even broken—will stop their banging and clashing.

So that when we cook and eat in a way that makes sense in our lives, that "sense" will refer to joy and also responsibility; and pleasure in eating will mean it is affordable and responsible; and responsibility will not be something that complicates the equation, but what keeps the sensible and the sensuous bound.

For this melding to happen, we'll have to start lifting the labels off things. I don't mean just of food itself, too much of which is made by companies that insist on corrupting honest ingredients, then brand the concoctions with meaningless names, like "jungle-berry bars," "barbecue chicken Caesar wraps," and "artisan ciabatta buffalo sliders."

I mean the alleviation of really useless abstractions that are everywhere.

For example, we will have to eat less meat, because the amount of it we eat now, whether raised on rich, fertile pastures or not, won't allow our water and soil to survive. But we will not feel pressure to be all of us vegetarians. With the state of our water sources and topsoil in mind, we will raise fewer animals; with the well-being of our bellies in mind, we will prepare their meat, and dishes around it, in ways that allow us to make the most of it. This will mean a small amount of meat will feed many mouths. Well-raised meat will be made more affordable, not just by necessary agricultural restructuring but by restructuring our culinary perspective.

Wiping our hands of the idea that meat means indulgent eating and vegetables virtuous eating, we will see that any eating can be indulgent, any virtuous, and any fine. Assuming vegetables continue to be what they are—more expensive and harder to come by than jungle-berry so-on, tragically perishable, and most nutritious grown nearby in soil where other animals or vegetables grow too—we will become experts at making the most of whatever vegetables we have at any point, in all senses, whether we are picking from a garden or a grocery store shelf.

We will sagely widen the scope of our larders to include what grows in nearby woods or sides of roads or between sidewalk cracks, and the hardy lamb's-quarters and herbs that we find flourishing on city blocks, combined with the few precious mushrooms that spring up under tall trees after a rain, will round our meals out nicely.

We will eschew recipes that send us chasing after ingredients, and instead cook what is already there, deliberately, in some olive oil or butter, or whatever fat our culinary heritage likes, or even just plain but economical water, with whole cloves of garlic and the right amount of salt.

We will find ourselves cooking several meals at once, and keeping the third of our food we throw away now—not out of piety, but the desire to keep eating well. We will use leftover meat, or vegetable flavored oil or butter, or even improved water the following day. And whether we have done it in one sitting or over a few, our food will have been savored slowly. This process and outlook will apply regardless of season and social stature.

The illusive idea of sustainable food *items* will fade into the far more practical, this-worldly idea of sustainable *ways* about food.

For this to happen, for practices to take the place of purchases, many more of us will need to know how to do simple, useful things: boil and roast, use salt, acid, fat, and heat. Others of us will find we like, in addition to all that, to grow herbs or dry chilies over the stove. We will, in short, learn and wield kitchen skill to make the right decisions easy, and make them taste good.

Because what is practical, pleasurable, and responsible changes each day, so will the details of our meals. Like a boat moored, they will naturally rise and fall with the tides. Here is a version of the graceful bobbing and tilting they will do:

Monday breakfast: a slice of yesterday's loaf of hard, dark bread, cut thick, toasted, drizzled with olive oil and honey, lovely if it's from nearby, still good at being thick and sweet if it's from elsewhere; or the last of some garlicky vegetables on the toast, if breakfast is a salty meal for you.

Monday lunch: a piece of baked omelet, which took you

ten minutes to make on Saturday, from the last of Friday's boiled potatoes and Thursday's roasted onion; a salad of roasted beets and pickled onions; an apple if it is autumn, little oranges if winter, strawberries if spring; or, regardless of season, a container of plain whole-milk yogurt, drizzled with a little more honey and raisins.

Monday that awful hungry time between lunch and dinner: a cup of mint tea, fresh or dried, walnuts, or yogurt with walnuts, or yogurt with peanut butter, and if you are me, probably all three.

Monday dinner: Sunday evening's beans, loved equally whether they've come from a trellis or from a can, warmed with bits of bacon and pork shoulder from Friday; topped with a fried egg gotten from the nice people next door, if you live in Berkeley or Brooklyn, or at the nearest farmers' market (of which there will be more, nearer!), where two dozen can be bought at once and kept for a whole month; a bowl of collard greens, sautéed with garlic and chili; a room-temperature salad made of odds and ends and pickled onions; more fresh fruit, or some figs, warmed up in some red wine; and a dollop of ricotta or goat's cheese.

Instead of making a sacrifice of what is good for what is right, or what is expensive for what is cheap, we will just pay attention to how lucky we are to be able to make simple, delicious things from what we have. Then we will be more willing and able to look critically and fluidly at the whole complex quilt of our eating: how we pay our workers, how we raise our food, and how we raise ourselves and each other.

Tamar Adler has worked as a chef, magazine editor, and cooking teacher. The author of An Everlasting Meal: Cooking with Economy and Grace, *she lives in Brooklyn, New York.*

GINGER STRAND

HUMILITY

Not long ago, the media got fired up about physics. Researchers at the CERN laboratory in Switzerland had shot some neutrinos toward an underground observatory in Italy, and evidence seemed to indicate that they traveled there faster than the speed of light. Yet according to Einstein's theory of relativity—on which much of modern physics depends—nothing travels faster than the speed of light. Members of the commentariat were exultant. Back to the drawing board, physicists! You've got a century's worth of equations to redo!

The physicists were surprisingly unruffled. Their attitude? Perhaps we did something wrong. Here's our data; please check our work. Oh, and would someone else please do the experiment again and see if you get the same result? "The potentially great impact of the result motivates the continuation of our studies," the CERN group wrote.

It might seem surprising that some of the world's top scientists were willing to allow that a few subatomic particles may have just undone a century's worth of physics. It might seem even more surprising they were equally willing to admit they could be mistaken. But their attitude was steeped in the true spirit of inquiry: a spirit that seeks answers without believing it already has them, and without overestimating its abilities to produce them.

There's only one word to describe this attitude: *humility*. Yet to call this virtue undervalued in our narcissistic culture would be a considerable understatement. We have become a nation of self-promoters, blogging and tweeting the details of our lives as if every heirloom tomato we consume were of national import. We teach our children self-confidence but neglect to encourage modesty. Our national motto has devolved to "We're number one." And our domestic politics have morphed into a partisan smackdown in which the idea of a political figure expressing doubt or uncertainty, as many once routinely did, has become laughable in the extreme. We have always been prone to technical hubris, but our confidence in our technology has reached new heights. Credible people can now argue that we are capable of geoengineering the planet, or that the coming "singularity"—in which we merge with our machines—will conquer death.

This lack of humility carries a high price: stultification. Because oddly, our conviction that we can do everything makes it hard to do anything. It takes humility to admit we have a problem, and it also takes humility to work on solving it. Part of why it has become so hard to take action on climate change is that no one can guarantee a result. What if we tax carbon and the economy suffers? What if we shut down our coal plants and the oceans still rise? What if we give research and development money to a solar company and it goes under? We seem to have lost the ability to try, fail, try again, fail better.

The CERN physicists are not paralyzed by uncertainty; they are motivated by it. Nor do they quake at the mere thought of error (they now believe that a poorly calibrated clock or a faulty cable between their GPS and their computer may have caused a measurement mistake). In the spirit of the scientific method, they recognize that the assumptions of the past may not be applicable to the future. They conduct their work with caution, with respect for the tradition in which they labor, with cooperation, and with willingness to fail. In short, with humility.

The root of *humility* is the Latin word *humus*, meaning "earth" or "ground." To have humility is to keep your feet on the ground, and also to recognize that the earth is where you end up. As humans, we all share the same fate: we die. After we accept this, we may be able to accept the rest of our limitations, to embrace the possibility of failure, and to join with each other in meeting the challenges posed by an uncertain future. It may sound simple, but it's not. Accepting limits while going on living is one of the hardest things humans do. One might say religions were created precisely for this purpose: to humble us. But science humbles us too, as does nature, if we pay attention. We must pay attention. Humility will keep us grounded as we move into the unknown.

Ginger Strand is an Orion *contributing editor and author of* Inventing Niagara: Beauty, Power, and Lies.

JULIA ALVAREZ

THE *WE* WAY
OF BEING

A COUPLE OF YEARS AGO, my husband, Bill, and I took two
trips far into the interior of rural Haiti from my native Dominican Republic. The first trip occurred six months before
the earthquake to attend the wedding of a young Haitian
friend, Piti; the second one took place six months after the
earthquake, when we returned with Piti and his young wife
and their baby to check in on their families. I did not know
that the poorest country in this hemisphere, and one of the
poorest in the world, would teach me so much about how to
live sustainably and joyfully on this planet.

Of the many lessons learned was how little we really need,
especially when we share what we have with others. Take the
wedding we attended. In that desolate and impoverished area of
northwest Haiti, no household owned more than a few chairs,
including that of the bride's parents. But since each local guest
arrived carrying one or two chairs, there were plenty of places to
sit, especially if we took turns. After sitting for a while, you sur-
rendered your chair. It actually felt good to stand up for a spell.

On the second trip we brought a whole pickup of supplies
for Piti's family and that of his new wife, Eseline. We un-

loaded the cargo at a friend's house because that's where the dirt road ended. Piti made three piles: one for the two families and one for his friend. How could he divvy up his riches and not include his friend? I learned that this was the basic investment plan in the community: you save what you have by sharing it. Later, when you find yourself in need, those you shared with will share with you.

Most of the time this actually works. When Piti's mother got sick, all those who had recently endured the same stomach flu pooled together their medicines and whatever knowledge they had garnered from the care they got, perhaps in some rural clinic or, for those who had made the trek, to hospitals in the closest cities of Gros Morne or Port-de-Paix. It reminds me of a comment by the Dominican environmental activist and revolutionary Aniana Vargas. In the early eighties, I spent a week interviewing her in the mountains of the Dominican Republic. When I assured her that I would give her credit whenever I quoted one of her ideas, she shrugged. It was not necessary. "Todo lo que se sabe en el mundo se sabe entre todos." All the knowledge in the world is a sum of what we all know put together.

But that attitude of shared wisdom must be extended to other resources: food and shelter and medical care. If we practiced this approach on a global scale and divvied out the goods so everyone had enough, no one would have less than enough.

The Xhosa people in South Africa have a word, *ubuntu*, which translates: "I am because you are." The ancient Mayans recognized a similar truth in the phrase *en lak ech*, which means "you are the other me." It's a way of thinking about ourselves as interconnected. We cannot exist in any meaningful way without each other.

As we look to the future, we need to look back to places like Haiti to learn how to use our resources wisely. Our capitalist societies are geared toward competition, scoring above someone else, owning bigger and better than our neighbor. But in those very places we've left behind in the dust, those underdeveloped, impoverished societies, which are already having to learn to survive with a lot less than we have, we might find some luminous and critical piece of information we will need to survive.

Julia Alvarez has written about this and other lessons learned in her new nonfiction book, A Wedding in Haiti.

ANDREW REVKIN

THE
KNOWOSPHERE

IT IS EASY TO BE DISCOURAGED about the prospects for advancing human progress while limiting environmental losses. The world appears to be in for a long period when money for almost any initiative in environmental conservation, education, even energy innovation, will be hard to come by. American politics is largely paralyzed. China is keener to sustain and expand its middle class than to limit coal use, while India, demographically, is preparing to be this century's China.

But these very conditions provide the perfect moment for a burst of bottom-up progress, driven by the extraordinary efficiency and impact that can come from using the web and other communication tools to connect an idea, expertise, or design with a glaring need. I've seen the potential in a host of arenas, from environmental education to disaster preparedness.

There's been a long-running race between the potency of human beings and our awareness, but the fast-expanding "knowosphere"—the interlaced, light-speed, super-cheap fabric of information and discourse enveloping the physical planet—can propel awareness into the lead for good. The knowosphere is the build-out of the more abstract concept of "noosphere"—a planet of the mind—developed in the early twentieth century by Vladimir Vernadsky, a Russian geochemist, Pierre Teilhard de Chardin, a French theologian, and others. The roots of such thinking go back as far as Darwin, who in *The Descent of Man*, in 1871, foresaw unity and empathy building through expanded awareness:

> *As man advances in civilization, and small tribes are united into larger communities, the simplest reason would tell each individual that he ought to extend his social instincts and sympathies to all the members of the same nation, though personally unknown to him. This point being once reached, there is only an artificial barrier to prevent his sympathies extending to the men of all nations and races.*

The artificial barrier is being breached by the web and related technologies. Of course there's plenty of potential for the web to amplify falsehoods, foment hatred, and facilitate violence, but I see the upside of connectedness completely swamping the darker possibilities.

Larry Kilham, an inventor and writer, says the key to the knowosphere is its ability to facilitate collective intelligence, a trait that "goes back to the cavemen who sat around the campfire and shared ideas about which spear head worked best on the hunt." As he put it, "With the advent of Internet forums, wikis, affinity groups, blogospheres, and so on we are into collective intelligence with a vengeance." I couldn't agree more. The vast divide between knowledge and skills, created by costly closed systems of communication and learning, is evaporating. There's no concrete barrier now preventing a student in a rural Kenyan village from listening to or watching a lecture on solar technology at the Massachusetts Institute of Technology. As a result of the opportunities presented by the knowosphere, my own work has largely shifted from journalism to seeking ways to build a loose network of schools and other institutions with the goal of facilitating such connectedness.

While at a meeting on the island of Nantucket on coastal issues related to climate change, I ran into a small team of British educators from a nonprofit group called Atlantic Rising. They were on the beach, working with students to chart what a meter of sea-level rise would mean for that place. They've done the same thing around the Atlantic Ocean, in both prosperous and poor communities, not only building awareness of environmental change but also, through Skype, building relationships between schools in coastal communities from Ghana to Scotland. This shows the power, through networked learning, to combine direct experience in nature with globe-spanning relationships. Imagine if the annual "BioBlitzes" held around the United States were part of a global BioBlitz in which students around the world posted and compared their findings online. Fast-advancing improvements in translation algorithms will soon largely eliminate language barriers, rendering moot the old goal of spreading the adoption of Esperanto, a common language.

Another example came through my ongoing reporting on efforts to gird poor communities against the worst impacts from earthquakes and other disasters. After the devastating loss of hundreds of schools and their students in Sichuan Province, I wrote about a simple design innovation conceived by Santiago Pujol, an earthquake engineer at Purdue, for building sturdier schools using the same materials already common in developing countries, but just configured differently. I would love to find ways to have that design available in every corner of the world where communities are building schools at a frantic pace to keep up with the cresting number of children on the planet—a billion teenagers and a billion younger students.

When asked about global trends and human prospects, I used to call myself a "despairing optimist," taking that term from the work of one of my heroes, René Dubos. These days, largely for the reasons I've articulated here, I drop the adjective.

Andrew Revkin is the Senior Fellow for Environmental Understanding at Pace University and writes the Dot Earth blog for the Op-Ed section of the New York Times.

JOSEPH BRUCHAC

CHILDREN WHO FEEL AT HOME ON THE EARTH

UNLIKE THE GENERATIONS BEFORE THEM, most of our children are strangers to nature. Doomed, some gloomy observers say, to be overweight, poorly socialized, self-centered. Their lives seem focused entirely on indoor pursuits. Passive watching, virtual reality, and Facebook "friending" have taken the place of physical interaction with the environment outside their air-conditioned boxes. Looking to the future, we have an opportunity to replace this new paradigm of isolation with an older, more sustainable, and more nurturing one. It is a way that American Indian children were not just taught about but immersed in, a path that fosters a participatory relationship with the planetary ecosystem of which we are all part. Although concerted efforts were made by the governments of the United States and Canada to destroy our traditional native ways of teaching and learning, they still exist and have a lot to offer anyone who is interested in helping young people feel supported by, intimate with, and at home in the natural world.

At the root of it are stories that tell of how we came from

the earth—which is not mere soil, but the source of our existence. In many Native American languages, we refer to the earth with words like *Nihima*, in Navajo, best translated into English as "Our Mother." The Iroquois Thanksgiving Address is spoken at the start of important gatherings, and many native ceremonies begin by giving thanks to the Mother Earth for providing us with all that we need in order to live. In our stories, dirt is not "dirty," it is life. (My Abenaki grandfather often said, "Everyone's got to eat a ton of dirt.") This is instructive because, as we now know, a lack of contact with the soil in a child's early years—an effect of the overly hygenic lifestyle we see everywhere today—appears to make that child more susceptible to infections late in life.

Kita. Listen. We all have two ears and only one mouth. We must listen twice as much as we talk. And as we listen, we may learn. There is an old saying among the Anishinabe: the more we know, the less we will fear. Listening is a path to that sort of intimate knowledge. It takes us out of ourselves, makes us aware of and connects us to the life around us. It is said by many of our elders that we learned to sing together by following the example of the wolves, who join their voices on the hilltops at night. Compositions played on the native flute are often inspired by the songs of the birds. When a child learns to listen to the music in nature, that child feels a closeness with the natural world and a desire to learn from it.

Of course there is danger in the natural world, and one must always show respect and be aware, but the right kind of knowledge provides safety. There are many stories told among our indigenous nations about children who become lost in the forest. But instead of being afraid, those children turn to their knowledge of the earth. They know where to take shelter, how to find food and water, how to make fire. Instead of being a threat to their safety—as we see in far too many modern films—the earth provides for them and safeguards them. In some cases, they are even helped by the animals of the forest, as in a Menominee story where a little girl lost in a winter storm is discovered sleeping in the den of a hibernating mother bear. The lessons of such stories are not, perhaps, that mother bears are waiting to care for our children. But the metaphor embodies the fundamental truth that those who have learned to listen to and understand the natural world are engaged in a reciprocal relationship with it: one helps the other, and in due course the help is returned.

Seeing oneself as a part of nature, learning and growing from that perspective, is a worldview that developed over the ages among indigenous cultures. Yet it still can be learned by the children of the future through exploring traditional native teachings, listening to nature, and then walking with care—but without fear—in the forest. Then each step that our children take may lead them toward a more native, healthful, and sustainable way of seeing and being.

Joseph Bruchac is a writer and traditional storyteller. His many books include the memoir At the End of Ridge Road, *which explores the links between his Abenaki Indian ancestry and his views on nature and social justice.*

PETE SEEGER

A DIFFERENT
KIND OF GROWTH

MORE THAN ANYTHING, I think we're going to need a sense
of humor to deal with the future we're facing. Because unless
we solve the problem of how we grow, there's a serious possibility there won't be a human race in a hundred years. A lot
of economists say, "You must grow, or you die." I once had an
argument with a local politician about this. I said, "The Hudson Valley is doubling every twenty years. We've got to slow
down." He said, "Pete, if you don't grow, you die." I sat up in
bed at one a.m. that night and thought: if it's true that if you
don't grow, you die, doesn't it follow that the quicker we grow,
the sooner we die?

This world is only so big. If we come to the point where
we have to grow or die, we'll die because we can't grow forever. Too much growth will be the death of us. Imagine what
this beautiful world would look like if for every one person
there were a thousand people. Obviously, you could hardly live
here. I sing a song about this with children.

Two times two is four!
Two times four is eight!

Two times eight is sixteen
And the hour is getting late!

We'll all be a-doubling, a-doubling, a-doubling
We'll all be a-doubling in thirty-two years.
We'll all be a-doubling, a-doubling, a-doubling
We'll all be a-doubling in thirty-two years.

(Sing after next two verses. It's fun.)

Two times sixteen is thirty-two,
Twice that is sixty-four;
Next comes a hundred twenty-eight,
And do you need to hear more?

(chorus)

Next comes two hundred fifty-six,
Next five hundred and twelve;
Next, one thousand twenty-four,
Figure it out yourself.

(chorus)

Keep doubling ten generations,
You'll have ancestors over a million.
Keep going another twenty,
You'll have ancestors over a trillion.

"Hold on!" I say. There never were a trillion people in the world—at least not yet. So some of our ancestors must have married cousins. That means you and I are all distant cousins of each other, no matter the color of our skins or the shape of our eyes. Then I get into the thing of what will happen in the future: can we keep on a-doubling?

> *Either people are going to have to get smaller*
> *Or the world's going to have to get bigger;*
> *Or there's a couple other possibilities,*
> *I'll leave it to you to figure.*

It's kind of funny when thirty little kids are all singing the chorus *a-doubling, a-doubling, a-doubling, a-doubling* at the same time.

This idea of staying small is all over the country now. It's not the majority yet, but it is being listened to. The agricultural revolution took thousands of years. The industrial revolution took hundreds of years. But the information revolution is only taking decades. If we use the information available to us, and use the brains God gave us, who knows what miracles may happen?

I have another song, "Arrange and Rearrange." It's about hoping our children have a future.

> *Sometimes I wake in the middle of the night,*
> *and rub my aching old eyes.*
> *Is this a voice from inside my head,*
> *or does it come down from the skies?*
> *There's a time to laugh, there's a time to weep,*
> *a time to make big change.*
> *Wake up you bum, the time has come:*
> *To arrange rearrange and rearrange.*
> *Oh-wee, oh-wye, to rearrange and rearrange and rearrange.*
>
> *Perhaps the biggest change will come,*
> *when we don't have to change much at all.*
> *When maniacs holler, "Grow, grow, grow,"*

> *we can choose to be small.*
> *The key word may be little,*
> *We only have to change a little bit.*
> *Eat a little food, drink a little drink,*
> *and only have to shit a little shit.*
> *Oh-wee, oh-wye, and only have to shit a little shit.*
>
> *Early in the mornin' when I see the sun,*
> *I say a little prayer for the world.*
> *I hope all the little children live a long, long time,*
> *Yes, every little boy and little girl.*
> *I hope they learn to laugh at the way*
> *Some wicked old words seem to change,*
> *'Cause that's what life's all about:*
> *To arrange and rearrange and rearrange.*
> *Oh-wee, oh-wye, to rearrange and rearrange and rearrange.*

I say to the children in the audience that I've given up on grownups, but I'm not giving up on them if they sing with me. *Sing it!* I say. Children like to sing.

Here's another song I've taught to a bunch of kids. God is in every verse:

> *When we sing with younger folks, we can never give up*
> *hope*
> *God's counting on me, God's counting on you*
> *Hopin' we'll all pull through, Hoping we'll all pull through,*
> *Hopin' we'll all pull through*
> *Me and you.*

That great mathematician Alfred North Whitehead, he had a very interesting definition of God. He said that the present holds within itself the complete sum of existence, forward and backward, that great amplitude of time which is eternity. So, if you're thinking of eternity, you're thinking about God. If I clap my hands, that's because all eternity told me to clap my hands. Likewise, when I clap my hands, I disturb molecules, which disturbs other molecules, which disturbs other molecules for all eternity to come. So, there you have God. I'll tell that to my crowd, and I get the whole of them singing . . .

> *Whatever God may mean to you, there's great work we*
> *need to do.*
> *God's counting on me, God's counting on you*

And then, we all sing that nice little chorus. You can sing it in your head, or you can tap your feet. You can clap your hands:

> *Hopin' we'll all pull through, Hoping we'll all pull through,*
> *Hopin' we'll all pull through*
> *Me and you.*

Pete Seeger is a renowned folk singer, environmental activist, and author of Where Have All the Flowers Gone: A Singalong Memoir.

CARL SAFINA

AN ENERGY
FUTURE

HERE'S WHAT WE KNOW: Though odorless and nontoxic
(indeed, our bodies produce and exhale it), the mushroom-
ing cloud of carbon dioxide going into the atmosphere has
turned into the most life-threatening pollutant in the history
of humankind. Our incessant burning of oil, coal, and gas has
unleashed into the atmosphere carbon that had been locked
away from the living world for hundreds of millions of years.
There's a third more carbon dioxide in the air than there was
when the first steam engines sparked the Industrial Revolution around 1800. We've created an enormous change to the
atmosphere in the blink of a geological eye.

Just a few of the more obvious ways this is poised to create havoc: warming and extreme weather are lowering global
grain yields and threatening the productivity of the world's
major crops and agricultural areas; warming is disrupting
the distribution of animals worldwide, separating some (such
as polar bears and certain whales) from their food supply;
warming is also causing a decline in ocean plankton densi-
ties, lowering the potential of the ocean to produce fish and
other wildlife and to recover from overfishing; melting ice

is raising sea levels, causing abandonment of some island nations and threatening to displace tens of millions of people living in coastal cities worldwide, which in turn threatens the peace (such as there is) as well as the futures of the cities themselves; acidification of the ocean is slowing coral growth and killing larval oysters in commercial hatcheries; at present trends, later in this century the acidifying ocean will begin *dissolving* the world's coral reefs.

Ever since I was in high school we've known that our thirst for oil is a national security threat, yoking us to unsavory dictators and political regimes who at times loathe us and frequently are loathsome. And anyway, oil and gas are getting harder to find because there's not enough to last forever. That's why we're no longer drilling for oil in Pennsylvania but are getting it from thousands of feet under the seafloor instead, in water a mile or more deep. Or fracturing the very bedrock in a gas-getting attempt that threatens the water supply of insignificant little towns such as New York City. These are desperate times.

So what do we need? Back in high school I learned that we need a diverse array of energy sources like solar panels on all our sun-reflecting roofs, and we also need to harness the wind, the tides, the heat of the earth—in short, we need to run civilization with the eternal forces that actually power the planet. We knew that then.

So what do we have? Congress recently rejected an attempt to take away the tens of billions of dollars of tax-fed subsidies that we shovel to the most profitable industry in the history of the world: Big Oil. This in a time when the Tea Party and the last remaining mainstream Republicans—if there are any—all scream for "tax relief." Turns out they're not serious. Why? Because Big Energy, fed like sumo wrestlers on our tax money while the true energy entrepreneurs starve, has installed congressional members who represent its interests rather than the public interest and any interest whatsoever in the future of our civilization. Then Big Energy uses more of our tax money to hire legions of lobbyists to keep it that way, while it turns public opinion against science, against new energy technology, and against ourselves. Repeat, ad infinitum. By making it impossible to create an energy future over the last four decades, Big Energy has left us stuck in the past, worshipping a form of energy that has no future, that is literally and figuratively dead, an energy path whose one key truth is in its name: fossil fuels.

Survival will depend on realizing that relying on dwindling, outmoded, and lethal forms of energy leaves us no future. We need a new, vibrant, living energy future that harnesses, rather than hurts, the planet's driving powers and our prospects.

Carl Safina is founding president of Blue Ocean Institute at Stony Brook University. His books include Song for the Blue Ocean *and* The View From Lazy Point: A Natural Year in an Unnatural World.

RALPH NADER

AN END TO CORPORATISM

CORPORATISM is the dominant controlling framework of government's functions, budgets, domestic and foreign politics, and appointments. Giant multinational corporations are willing to spend whatever it takes on electoral campaigns and to devote their command of mass media toward corporatizing our society. These corporate giants, as artificial legal entities, have almost all the constitutional rights of real people. In addition, their ever-expanding privileges and immunities make a mockery of equal justice under the law between real people and the ExxonMobils, Pfizers, Aetnas, Monsantos, Citibanks, and Lockheed Martins.

Corporatism—that is, the corporate state—and democracy are also incompatible. According to the most celebrated free-market philosophers and theorists, corporatism, with its concentration of power, is incompatible with both conservatism and liberalism. In a message to Congress in 1938 to establish a commission on concentrated corporate power, President Franklin D. Roosevelt called the control of government by private economic power "fascism." The "public sentiment," to use Abraham Lincoln's felicitous phrase, is overwhelmingly opposed to unbridled corporate power. A

Businessweek poll back in September 2000 showed that over 70 percent of the respondents thought corporations had too much control over their lives; this was eight years before the criminals and gamblers on Wall Street crashed our economy into steep recession, millions of home foreclosures, mass unemployment, shredded pensions and investments, and trillions of dollars in taxpayer bailouts.

Corporatism is actively taking away our fundamental rights of civil jury remedies for wrongful injuries (with so-called tort reform), freedom to negotiate contracts (curtailed by those mandatory fine-print contracts that we must all sign), the freedom to bargain collectively as workers (with union-busting), our national sovereignty when it comes to protecting our economy (with NAFTA and World Trade Organization agreements that pull down our workers' living standards), and, most basically, our need to subordinate commercial values to the far more critical civic values that constitute a just society.

The struggle to end corporatism and rebuild our democracy will be centered on Congress—the most powerful branch of government under our Constitution and the one that could be the most responsive to corporate-accountability activists, and most readily repopulated with corporate-reform representatives. Roughly fifteen hundred large corporations get their way with most of the 535 members of the House and Senate. Yet, these companies, while they have money and power, don't have a single vote. The people have all the votes. Voters need to be consistently informed about the adverse effects of corporations on their livelihoods, their taxes, their peace, their children, and their environment.

Today a huge civic vacuum exists that can be filled with organized Congress watchers and advocates. Imagine 535 citizen groups, equipped with a broadly supported corporate accountability agenda, becoming a decisive critical mass. Included in this agenda are the following:

- Comprehensive corporate law enforcement reform

- Subordination of corporations, all chartered into existence by state authority, to the sovereignty of the people under our Constitution

- Displacement of corporate supremacy by expanding community economies (such as more democratic credit unions, local farmer-to-consumer markets, community health and prevention clinics, local, renewable, and efficient energy production, and local participatory sports and arts)

To make this work, each congressional district averaging 650,000 persons will need the following: 2,000 citizens each pledging $100; 200 or more coordinated volunteer hours a year; four full-time staff; and links to other allied groups across the land. This focused civic power can turn the tide in Congress toward enforceable and enduring corporate reform, subordination of corporations, abolition of corporate personhood, and significant sales displacement by competitive community businesses.

A billionaire or two alone could kick-start this grand shift of power reasserting the sovereignty of the people. Note that our Constitution begins with the words "we the people," not "we the corporations." There is no mention whatsoever of the words *corporation* or *company* in the entire Constitution. Then why do they control us? Why are they our masters instead of our servants, as they were authorized to be by the early state legislatures of our republic? A shift of power away from the few who now decide for the many will reverse the steady decay of our weakening democracy and the decline of our economy, our earning power, our public works, our public educational institutions, and our global role in advocating for peace and environmental preservation. It is essential to the survival of democracy itself.

Ralph Nader is a consumer advocate, former presidential candidate, and author of the new book Getting Steamed to Overcome Corporatism: Build It Together to Win.

PAUL KINGSNORTH

IMPROVISATION

So, THE CLIMATE IS FILLING UP with carbon and methane,
the forests are falling, the seas are emptying. The human
population continues to expand, along with its appetites.
Everything is converging toward an implosion.

The only way to prevent this from happening is by making a plan. A really big plan—bigger than any plan has ever
been. This plan is going to have to apply to the entire earth
and everyone on it. It is going to have to measure and control
how much we consume and emit, and tightly regulate how we
live. It is going to have to be agreed upon by all governments,
which in turn are going to have to persuade their populations.
It is going to have to involve radical and rapid technological
change alongside radical and rapid lifestyle change. It's going to have to happen within the next thirty years max, or it's
game over.

Or so I keep hearing, from all sorts of people. From
mainstream environmentalists, from soft-left politicians, from
"sustainability consultants," from think tanks, from despera-
does and idealists everywhere. Only a plan can save us now.

It's an understandable reaction, in some ways. It's also
absurd. It's been twenty years since the first Earth Summit.
Can anybody count the number of plans to "save the planet"

that have emerged in those two decades? The books, reports, commissions, treaties? Yet you won't even need the fingers on one hand to count the number of them that have been put into place.

Plans—big plans, anyway—do not generally work, which is a great relief. Think about what the world could end up looking like if a Global Uber-plan to Save Civilization and Nature were put in place:

> *Densely populated, centrally controlled, nuclear-powered, computer-directed, firmly and thoroughly policed. Call it the Anthill State, the Beehive Society, a technocratic despotism . . .*

That was Edward Abbey's vision of the future if our civilization continued on its trajectory. It is the vision that environmentalism came into being to challenge. And it is now, ironically, the direction in which the logic of carbon reduction, "sustainability," and top-down planet-saving "plans" are driving us.

Ivan Illich would not have been surprised by this; neither would E. F. Schumacher or Leopold Kohr. They knew that the techno-industrial mindset that created mass societies was not a useful corrective to the problems it had caused. Before the mainstream environmental movement forgot its origins in convivial and human-scale approaches and began to cleave to the holy trinity of Big Tech, Big Politics, and Big Science, it would have been clear enough: We do not need a plan. What we need is to learn how to improvise; how to let go. The future will not be controlled. We are not going to stop climate change with international treaties or a rollout of turbines and reactors. We are not going to prevent ecocide through the work of government or a rising of the people. We are not going to save ourselves with microsolar or giant space mirrors.

The future, like most of the past, is going to be improvised. On a practical level, the most useful skills are likely to be coping with poverty, building a measure of self-sufficiency and self-reliance, and working as a member of a community. On a more intellectual, or perhaps metaphysical, level, the most useful skill looks to me to be the ability to question our stories. The ability to ask what progress is, what we mean by *nature* and *civilization*, how we can grow in ways other than the material, how we can live well without relying on machines that are destined to destroy the planet in order to save it.

Improvisation, then: flexibility, a willingness to give things up, the ability to fall and land with some measure of grace. I'm placing my bets on even the best-laid plans falling through. I can live with uncertainty. Can you?

Paul Kingsnorth is a writer, recovering environmentalist, and founder of the Dark Mountain Project.

CHRISTOF MAUCH

HINDSIGHT

HISTORIANS DON'T SAVE LIVES like doctors; they don't build bridges like engineers, and they don't console like preachers. But without history, our future would be empty and incomprehensible. History empowers us by making sense of the past. It can give us a glimpse of what might happen, or what will happen if we repeat past mistakes, and it can remind us of our power to change the world for the better.

Today, as deserts spread, glaciers melt, and our planet's population relentlessly rises, there is no history more important than environmental history. It helps us understand the relationship between nature and culture over time, and forces us to ask new questions, such as how have past natural disasters changed the fate of cultures? The eruption of a volcano in 1600 BC, for example, led to the downfall of the thriving Minoan culture and provided an opening for the Greeks, and later, the Romans, Portuguese, and Spanish, to dominate the Mediterranean.

Clearly, actors other than humans have had an enormous impact on history. Even the tiny mosquito—and the diseases that it carries, malaria and yellow fever—has played a starring role. These seemingly insignificant creatures may have been more decisive in the struggle for American independence than George Washington's troops. Likewise, an adaptive resistance to mosquito attacks helped the Spanish keep their empire from European rivals for centuries. History thus reminds us that not everything on this planet can be controlled by humans.

And yet, there is much that humans have altered on the face of this earth, and quickly too. How many millions of years did nature take to produce fossil fuels, and in what microscopic period of time will humans use them up? How many millions of acres of arid land are transformed into a desert, year after year, through shortsighted land use? Mother Nature doesn't clear land for cultivation, nor draw up land development plans, and she doesn't legislate on energy use. She produces oil, fertile lands on which crops can grow, and provides water. Humans have enormous leeway for their own actions. What we on this planet make of our environment is to a large degree our own affair and is closely connected to the way we understand our history. There are plenty of lessons from the past—warnings, to be sure—but also models for success.

How might we perceive our future if we recognize that there is no straightforward trajectory in the relationship between humanity and nature, but rather a state of flux, of give and take between two actors? A few thousand years ago, Chinese people migrated to an area that used to be covered by the ocean, and they established great cities like Suzhou and Shanghai. Now, water threatens to take back cities across the globe. The challenge for humanity is one of adaptation to unpredictable fissures in the seam between human and natural actions.

And what looks like progress from one perspective may in reality be a step backward. The tragedy unleashed by Hurricane Katrina teaches us that we cannot protect ourselves from floodwaters by building stronger dams and higher levees. Hurricane Betsy, which struck New Orleans in 1965, was one of the most powerful storms ever to hit the United States, and yet there were far fewer casualties. Earlier generations were better prepared. Rather than staving off the inevitable, they adjusted to it by building houses on higher ground, providing a network of public transportation for evacuation, and establishing a dense network of shelters throughout the city. With the benefit of hindsight, we now know that future measures against disaster need to look more like efforts from fifty years ago.

As the future unfolds, the interplay between human and natural action and reaction will continue to yield unpredictable conditions, and call for new forms of adaptation. It may help to draw on the wisdom of Søren Kierkegaard, who reminded us that we must live our lives looking forward; but it is only by looking backward that we can understand them.

Christof Mauch directs the Rachel Carson Center for Environment and Society, a research institute for the environmental humanities based at Ludwig Maximilian University in Munich, Germany.

RUBÉN MARTÍNEZ

NEIGHBORLINESS

FOR THREE YEARS I lived in the northern New Mexican village of Velarde. The natural setting of the area is iconic—a
land that has been obsessively painted and photographed by
American artists for over a century. Velarde sits alongside the
Rio Grande, which is lined with a verdant cottonwood bosque.
Beyond the river to the west rises a dramatic black mesa of ba-
salt dotted with juniper. To the east, the snowcapped Truchas
Peaks of the Sangre de Cristo Mountains; to the southwest,
the massive girth of the Jemez range; to the north, the craggy
mouth of a canyon that opens into the awesome Rio Grande
Gorge. People often told me how lucky I was to call such a
remarkable landscape home.

The human geography of the Española Valley sharply
contrasted with the natural—the beauty colluding with ineq-
uity by hiding it. Velarde is part of Rio Arriba County, among
the poorest in New Mexico, which in turn is among the poorest states in the country. The Española Valley also lies at the
center of a rough triangle formed by Santa Fe, Taos, and Los
Alamos—the three richest cities in the state and among the
wealthiest in the nation. The disparity between the valley and
the affluent highlands is a perfect illustration of the "one" and
the "ninety-nine."

My wife, Angela, and I moved to Velarde to be close to the people who she was interviewing for her anthropology dissertation about the family ties that can sometimes enable heroin addiction and, at other times, provide the kind of succor that rehab can't. Although our neighbors in the village were not among the subjects of Angela's study, many of them fit the profile: young, poor, and addicted. The neighbors who most drew our attention lived in a charming adobe with a pitched tin roof, a house that is the very picture of New Mexican pastoral. They were a young family, a mother and a father and a toddler boy. The first words I heard from them were the mother shrieking at the father: "I WANT YOU THE FUCK OUT OF HERE!"

Angela and I saw the family steadily disintegrate during our time in the village. The fighting became more frequent. Their "business" grew—traffic pulled in and out of their driveway at all hours. There was at least one police raid that resulted in arrests. Eventually, there would be a death. And what did we do as all this happened next door to us? We watched. There was a window in our attic that looked down on their patio and front door. During their fights, we often sat at the window. Our neighbors never knew their drama had an audience.

It was extremely troubling to gaze upon our neighbors' lives this way, but that didn't stop us from looking through the window—surely projecting our own conflicts onto theirs. Angela and I often talked about what else we could or should do about the situation. Try to talk to the parents, urge them into drug rehab? Snitch on them? Should we have opened our door to the mother when she cried hysterically after a particularly nasty fight? We discarded all these possibilities because ultimately we felt that it was not our place to intervene, although a part of our reticence to become involved also resulted from a fear of repercussions. So we played by the rules, respecting the rigid borders that hold neighbors apart, even when people are most in need.

When death came to our neighbors' house, it made me question our rationalizations. It made me feel that I'd not only failed my neighbors, but also to live up to the ideals of solidarity and hospitality that imbued the articles and books that I wrote. I remain haunted by the idea that intervention had very much been our place after all.

Since Angela and I left Velarde in late 2006, drug-related violence has exploded in Mexico, our neighbor to the south, the homeland of my paternal grandparents that I have visited and occasionally lived in throughout my life. I was looking forward to sharing the place with our young twin daughters, but much of the Mexico that I've known and loved is too unstable for us to visit as a family today. We are cut off from these neighbors, too.

At least that is how I was feeling when in the spring of 2011, tragedy came to Javier Sicilia, one of Mexico's most highly regarded poets, whose son, who had no connection to drugs, was murdered in a cartel-related crime. Sicilia made his mourning public by staging marches and cross-country caravans in which he gathered large crowds of others who've lost loved ones. The death toll has surpassed sixty thousand in six years of conflict—with as many as twenty thousand "disappeared" and hundreds of thousands more displaced from their homes due to "inseguridad." Facing this landscape of loss, Sicilia invoked the colloquial Mexicanism "estamos hasta la madre" (we've had enough) to call for an end to the violence and impunity, which is itself the result of a particular relationship between neighbors— the supply of drugs in Mexico and the demand for them in the United States, weapons manufactured on this side of the border used to kill innocents on the other, the Obama administration's support for Felipe Calderón's "war on the drug cartels."

As I write this, Javier Sicilia is planning on bringing his Movimiento por la Paz con Justicia y Dignidad caravan from the border to Washington DC, symbolically uniting victims—a daughter in Juárez, a son in East LA—across the political line that separates them. My neighbors in Velarde were addicted to drugs that came across that line. As an American, I cannot shirk my responsibility for the blood spilled in Mexico. The borderless future of the borderlands is already here.

It is our place to intervene—on both sides now.

Rubén Martínez is the author of Desert America *and a professor of literature and writing at Loyola Marymount University.*

TERRY TEMPEST WILLIAMS

THE TELLURIAN

WE SMELLED THEM before we heard them. We heard them before we saw them. And when we saw them we disappeared in the eyes of kin. *Gorilla beringei beringei.*

Tellurian: of Earth. Inhabitants of Earth. In the Virunga Mountains of Rwanda, we walked with mountain gorillas. We followed them. We followed them through a wet bamboo forest, ducking and sliding as they moved powerfully, deliberately, gracefully through the landscape. It was a family of twenty-one individuals. We were a family of four with two guides. When they crossed over a stone fence, jumping down from the piled rocks of lava, we did the same. Without thought, we found ourselves standing on the steep slopes of potato fields.

The silverback turned toward us. We froze. My eyes looked down.

Our guide, Frances Ndagijimana, knows him by name. "Kwitonda." He is the dominant silverback. He sets the direction and the pace for the day. All females follow him. There are three other silverbacks, two blackbacks, the juveniles and babies, all moving through the rich black furrows of Irish potatoes. Our guide tells us that this is a hopeful story of how local communities from Ruhengeri to Kinigi have become conservationists and work with the gorillas. Everyone benefits.

The economy is growing.

It does not feel hopeful to me. It feels crowded and precarious. The bleeding of forest into field conceals a great wound. What is the wound? We never see the wound. But I smell it. Familiar. Draped in their bright batiked kitenges, the women with their hoes in hand scatter.

The silverback sits down and leans his great black body against the trunk of a tree and looks out over the vast expanse of quilted hills into the Congo where he and his clan once lived. The Congo is at war. Women are being raped. Forests are being burned. Gorillas are being killed. Charcoal is being sold. Kwitonda and his clan fled to the mountains of Rwanda in shrouds of smoke. Now, they are refugees. Exiled.

Meanwhile, Rwanda has been looking for oil, is thirsty for oil, and appears to have found it on the flanks of Virunga National Park. Kwitonda is now sitting on reserves of oil.

There is a gorilla in the room. What is it? The American artist Walton Ford's painting of him hangs in a room at the Paul Kasmin Gallery in New York City. It is large and harrowing and can be mistaken for a cartoon. It is not a cartoon, nor a parody. It is a portrait of King Kong. And it looks a lot like us.

And Ben Peberdy has created a collage titled "The Giant Buddha" that hangs on the rippled wall of the Main Street Museum in White River Junction, Vermont, where Hurricane Irene ripped through and flooded the town last summer. "The Giant Buddha" is another gorilla, only six inches tall, who holds a dancing atom serenely on his lap, captive to our atomic, demonic visions of the future. Neither Ford nor Peberdy's portrait shows this beast in its rightful place.

Of place: *Tellurian*.

Displacement is my concern. Disappearance is my fear. There is no home for those who are native, of Earth, inhabitants of Earth, anymore. *Tellurian* is an endangered word that every endangered species hides inside. We are all on the run, human and wild. Endangered. Exiled. Refugees.

I smell the wound and it smells like me. This wound will not heal and has spread as an infection. Stabbed by our illusions and legacies of grandeur, we stagger in our decaying forests of consumption. We are lost. We are in pain. And we don't know the cause of or the cure for what is making us sick. We long for something more when what we have is more than enough. We are becoming blind. We are becoming deaf. We are hobbling along the path of distractions, trying to find our way back or forward or sideways to a place of dreams.

What is the dream?

I wish there were a gorilla in every corner of our imaginations to remind us what we choose to both harm and ignore. I wish we could smell them, hear them, see them for who they are in real time and space, even know them by name: the most gentle of creatures, with authentic strength and power. But there are no gorillas in the rooms of our considerations— the boardrooms, the bedrooms from which we populate the world. Inside our sitting rooms, inside the halls of power and public policy there is only talking, endless talking, that generates schemes to dominate the world through a beautifully seductive phrase, "the American Dream." There is only our flimsy mythology of King Kong, of a man in a gorilla suit plucking airplanes from the New York City sky.

Terror is in the air.

We have forgotten what is true.

We have forgotten our genealogy.

We have forgotten the difference between fear and awe because to face the gaze of a gorilla is a privilege and rarity.

My family and I had one hour with Kwitonda's clan of mountain gorillas foraging among the bamboo shoots, leading us from the forest into the fertile fields of Rwanda, these refugees from the Congo, struggling to find peace. They smelled us before they heard us. They heard us before they saw us. And when they saw us, they stared briefly—then moved on.

Terry Tempest Williams is writer, naturalist, and environmental activist. Her most recent book is When Women Were Birds: Fifty-four Variations on Voice.

ACKNOWLEDGMENTS

SPECIAL THANKS to all those who contributed essays to this volume. Your thoughts are a gift; the sum of them an even greater one. Gratitude goes as well to the hundreds of writers and artists who have sustained a creative conversation in the pages of *Orion* over the past thirty years, not to mention our thousands of generous and loyal readers and donors.

Every member of the *Orion* staff helped to realize this project in one way or another. Special recognition goes to H. Emerson Blake, Andrew Blechman, Hannah Fries, Scott Gast, and Kristen Hewitt. Without their visioning and editorial support this book would not exist.

ABOUT ORION MAGAZINE

SINCE 1982, *Orion* has been a meeting place for people who seek a conversation about nature and culture that is rooted in beauty, imagination, and hope. Through the written word, the visual arts, and the ideas of our culture's most imaginative thinkers, *Orion* seeks to craft a vision for a better future for both people and planet.

Reader-supported and totally advertising-free, *Orion* blends scientific thinking with the arts, and the intellectual with the emotional. *Orion* has a long history of publishing the work of established writers from Wendell Berry, Terry Tempest Williams, and Barry Lopez to Rebecca Solnit, Luis Alberto Urrea, and Sandra Steingraber.

Orion is also grounded in the visual arts, publishing picture essays and art portfolios that challenge the traditional definition of "environment" and invite readers to think deeply about their place in the natural world. *Orion*'s website, www.orionmagazine.org, features multimedia web extras including slide shows and author interviews, as well as opportunities for readers to discuss *Orion* articles.

Orion is published bimonthly by The Orion Society, a nonprofit 501(c)3 organization, and is available in both print and digital editions.

Subscribe

Orion publishes six beautiful, inspiring issues per year. To get a free trial issue, purchase a subscription, or order a gift subscription, please visit www.orionmagazine.org/subscribe or call 888/254-3713.

Support

Orion depends entirely on the generous support of readers and foundations to publish the magazine and books like this one. To support *Orion*, please visit www.orionmagazine.org/donate, or send a contribution directly to *Orion* at 187 Main Street, Great Barrington, MA, 01230.

To discuss making a gift of stock or securities, or for information about how to include *Orion* in your estate plans, please call us at 888/254-3713, or send an e-mail to development@orionmagazine.org.

Shop

Head to the *Orion* website, www.orionmagazine.org, to purchase *Orion* books, organic cotton t-shirts, and other merchandise featuring the distinctive *Orion* logo. Back issues from the past thirty years are also available.

MORE BOOKS FROM ORION

ORION READERS

Orion Readers collect landmark *Orion* essays into short thematic volumes:

Change Everything Now. A selection of essays about ecological urgency.

Thirty-Year Plan: Thirty Writers on What We Need to Build a Better Future. An eloquent statement on the future of humanity.

Wonder and Other Survival Skills. A collection of thoughtful and inspirational writing on our relationship to the natural world.

Beyond Ecophobia: Reclaiming the Heart in Nature Education, by David Sobel. An expanded version of one of *Orion*'s most popular articles that speaks to those interested in nurturing in children the ability to understand and care deeply for nature from an early age.

Into the Field: A Guide to Locally Focused Learning, by Claire Walker Leslie, John Tallmadge, and Tom Wessels, with an introduction by Ann Zwinger. Curriculum ideas for teachers interested in taking their students out of doors.

Place-Based Education: Connecting Classrooms & Communities, by David Sobel. A guide for using the local community and environment as the starting place for curriculum learning, strengthening community bonds, appreciation for the natural world, and a commitment to citizen engagement.

ORION ANTHOLOGIES

Finding Home: Writing on Nature and Culture from Orion *Magazine,* edited by Peter Sauer. An anthology of the best writing from *Orion* published from 1982 to 1992.

The Future of Nature: Writing on a Human Ecology from Orion *Magazine,* selected and introduced by Barry Lopez. An anthology of the best writing from *Orion* published from 1992 to 2007.

FOR EDUCATORS

Ideal for reading groups and academic course adoption, many *Orion* books are accompanied by a downloadable teacher's guide consisting of key discussion questions. Teacher's guides can be found on the *Orion* website at www.orionmagazine .org/education.

Series design by Hans Teensma,
principal of the design studio Impress
(www.impressinc.com), which has
designed *Orion* since 1998.
The typeface is Scala, designed by Dutch
typographer Martin Majoor in 1990.
Printed by BookMobile.